WILDERNESS CANADA

"Development" continues. Canada's
standard of living, second highest in the
world,…is in no danger of losing that proud
position. Washing machines and television sets
abound.…Superhighways devour uncounted
acres of fertile land, and the second highest
incidence of automobiles achieves, in the
metropolitan areas, the second highest air
pollution. Ugly little towns prosper, all calling
themselves cities and all looking like faithful
copies of Omaha, Nebraska.

This is not a Canada to call forth any man's
love. But just north of it still lies a different
kind of land—too barren ever to be thickly
settled, too bleak to be popular like Blackpool
or Miami. There is no reason to doubt that
it will always be there, and so long as it is
there Canada will not die.

BLAIR FRASER: *The Search for Identity*

WILDERNESS CANADA

Edited by
BORDEN SPEARS

Photographs assembled by
BRUCE M. LITTELJOHN

Designed by
JON EBY

CLARKE, IRWIN & COMPANY LIMITED
TORONTO/VANCOUVER/1970

The publishers wish to thank the following companies for permission
to quote from their works:
Doubleday Canada Limited, from *The Search for Identity* by Blair Fraser;
Harold Matson Company, Inc., from *They Shall Inherit the Earth* by
Morley Callaghan, Copyright 1935, 1962 by Morley Callaghan.
Reprinted by permission of Harold Matson Company, Inc.;
Oxford University Press, from "The Lonely Land" by A.J.M. Smith

Fine Books Division
Maclean-Hunter Limited

Distributed in the United States
by E.P. Dutton & Co., Inc., New York
ISBN 0 525 23425 X

Printed in Canada

PREFACE

Most of Canada is wilderness, a fact of geography that makes it virtually unique among the "developed" countries. Other countries are what man has made them; Canadians, whether consciously or not, are a people shaped and conditioned in many special ways by the nature of the illimitable land itself.

In terms of geology, it is one of the planet's oldest regions; in terms of human history, among the youngest. Vast and silent, enigmatic and inhospitable, the wilderness extends from the southern fringe of settlement to the polar icecap. It is one of the great determining factors of our national experience, affecting our responses to the human situation.

This book is about the special meaning of the wilderness to the Canadian mind and spirit. It is not a book about natural wealth and resources and industrial potential. Neither does it treat the wilderness as escape, though it does conceive the continuing wilderness in some sense as a safety valve against the pressures of modern alienation.

The writers and photographers whose work the book contains are, for the most part, men of the cities. But they are also among the relatively few Canadians who know the wilderness at first hand; who have experienced its challenges, its rewards, its fascination for modern man. This book is their joint celebration of the wilderness they respect and cherish and which they now see threatened.

It is also a memorial to Blair Fraser, one of Canada's great journalists, an eloquent interpreter of political and social change, an embodiment in himself of the Canadian identity—and a man of the wilderness. Fraser was a trustee of the Quetico Foundation, a non-profit association dedicated to the preservation of wilderness areas, and a member of the Voyageurs, an informal group of vigorous adventurers who find their strenuous refreshment in retracing, by canoe, the ancient fur-trade routes that threaded the continent from Montreal to Athabasca and beyond.

It was in the Quetico Foundation that this book had its genesis. Blair Fraser died, in May 1968, when his canoe was swamped in the white waters of a northern river. His friends erected a stone cairn at the scene of the tragedy, but his associates in the Foundation sought also for a commemorative instrument which might communicate to many other Canadians his special passion for the wilderness they share. This book is the result.

Two of the contributors, Pierre Elliott Trudeau and Eric Morse, are men who paddled and portaged with Fraser. Morse, a wilderness traveller for fifty years, is an authority on the fur-trade routes. Of the other writers, Fred Bodsworth, naturalist and novelist, is an internationally known exponent of wilderness preservation. Professor George Woodcock is the founder-editor of *Canadian Literature* and a frequent contributor to art journals; he discusses the influence of the wilderness on Canadian literature and painting, from the explorers' journals to the Group of Seven and the present day. John A. Livingston, author and television producer, eloquently presents the case for conservation. R. Yorke Edwards, a specialist in the Canadian Wildlife Service, intimately knows the birds and animals of the north. Bruce West, author and newspaper columnist, grew up in an Ontario lumbering town and has never lost his fascination with the special breed of men the wilderness produces. And there is Blair Fraser's own account of a journey by canoe from Lake Superior to Fort Frances, along the route pioneered by Pierre de La Vérendrye in 1731.

Many persons have contributed, directly or indirectly, to *Wilderness Canada;* a very few special acknowledgements should be made. The Quetico Foundation furnished not only the initial inspiration, but also funds to launch and nourish the project. Its Chairman, John B. Ridley, provided support, encouragement and managerial skill at every stage, while scrupulously refraining from any attempt to influence the editorial direction. Of the Trustees, Dr. O. M. Solandt and Dr. A. H. J. Lovink took a close personal interest. Floyd S. Chalmers, then chairman of Maclean-Hunter Ltd., offered practical counsel.

Bruce M. Litteljohn, himself a wilderness historian and photographer, canvassed the continent's photographers to assemble what may well be the finest collection of wilderness pictures ever brought together. Finally, there is the work of Jon Eby as designer of the book, which speaks for itself.

Wilderness Canada is, to employ the current jargon, an "unstructured" book. It is not definitive; it has a theme but no propaganda message. It is *sui generis*. Its writers did not consult each other; if the book achieves a unity, that unity emerges from the writers' common desire to transmit their own shared feeling for the wilderness, and a common recognition that it was appropriate to do so in the name of a man who inspired their affection and respect.

Borden Spears
Toronto, 1970

THE PHOTOGRAPHERS

William D. Addison

Paul Baich—National Film Board

Robert W. Barnett

Fred Bruemmer

William I. Campbell

C. B. Cragg

Wayland Drew

Ken Dudley

John G. Foster

J.W.L. Goering

Jack Hasse

Ross B. Hodgetts

Norman R. Lightfoot

Bruce M. Litteljohn

William C. Mason

Steve Moss

Dalton Muir—National Parks

Michael Naughton

Randy Saylor

Robert R. Taylor

J. Wallace

Doug Wilkinson—National Film Board

Dr. Frank Wood

CONTENTS

WILDERNESS CANADA

PIERRE ELLIOTT TRUDEAU

Exhaustion and Fulfilment: The Ascetic in a Canoe

I would not know how to instil a taste for adventure in those who have not acquired it. (Anyway, who can ever prove the necessity for the gypsy life?) And yet there are people who suddenly tear themselves away from their comfortable existence and, using the energy of their bodies as an example to their brains, apply themselves to the discovery of unsuspected pleasures and places.

I would like to point out to these people a type of labour from which they are certain to profit: an expedition by canoe.

I do not just mean "canoeing." Not that I wish to disparage that pastime, which is worth more than many another. But, looked at closely, there is perhaps only a difference of money between the canoeists of Lafontaine Park and those who dare to cross a lake, make a portage, spend a night in a tent and return exhausted, always in the care of a fatherly guide—a brief interlude momentarily interrupting the normal course of digestion.

A canoeing expedition, which demands much more than that, is also much more rewarding.

It involves a starting rather than a parting. Although it assumes the breaking of ties, its purpose is not to destroy the past, but to lay a foundation for the future. From now on, every living act will be built on this step, which will serve as a base long after the return of the expedition...and until the next one.

What is essential at the beginning is the resolve to reach the saturation point. Ideally, the trip should end only when the members are making no further progress within themselves. They should not be fooled, though, by a period of boredom, weariness or disgust; that is not the end, but the last obstacle before it. Let saturation be serene!

So you must paddle for days, or weeks, or perhaps months on end. My friends and I were obliged, on pain of death, to do more than a thousand miles by canoe, from Montreal to Hudson Bay. But let no one be deterred by a shortage of time. A more intense pace can compensate for a shorter trip.

This essay, which was originally published in French in the November 1944 issue of JEC (*Jeunesse étudiante catholique*), appears here for the first time in translation.

What sets a canoeing expedition apart is that it purifies you more rapidly and inescapably than any other. Travel a thousand miles by train and you are a brute; pedal five hundred on a bicycle and you remain basically a bourgeois; paddle a hundred in a canoe and you are already a child of nature.

For it is a condition of such a trip that you entrust yourself, stripped of your worldly goods, to nature. Canoe and paddle, blanket and knife, salt pork and flour, fishing rod and rifle; that is about the extent of your wealth. To remove all the useless material baggage from a man's heritage is, at the same time, to free his mind from petty pre-occupations, calculations and memories.

On the other hand, what fabulous and undeveloped mines are to be found in nature, friendship and oneself! The paddler has no choice but to draw everything from them. Later, forgetting that this habit was adopted under duress, he will be astonished to find so many re-sources within himself.

Nevertheless, he will have returned a more ardent believer from a time when religion, like everything else, became simple. The impos-sibility of scandal creates a new morality, and prayer becomes a friendly chiding of the divinity, who has again become part of our everyday affairs. (My friend, Guy Viau, could say about our adven-ture, "We got along very well with God, who is a damn good sport. Only once did we threaten to break off diplomatic relations if he con-tinued to rain on us. But we were joking. We would never have done so, and well he knew it. So he continued to rain on us.")

The canoe is also a school of friendship. You learn that your best friend is not a rifle, but someone who shares a night's sleep with you after ten hours of paddling at the other end of a canoe. Let's say that you have to be towed up a rapid and it's your turn to stay in the canoe and guide it. You watch your friend stumbling over logs, slid-ing on rocks, sticking in gumbo, tearing the skin on his legs and drink-ing water for which he does not thirst, yet never letting go of the rope; meanwhile, safely in the middle of the cataract, you spray your hauler with a stream of derision. When this same man has also fed you ex-actly half his catch, and has made a double portage because of your injury, you can boast of having a friend for life, and one who knows you well.

How does the trip affect your personality? Allow me to make a fine distinction, and I would say that you return not so much a man who reasons more, but a more reasonable man. For, throughout this time, your mind has learned to exercise itself in the working condi-tions which nature intended. Its primordial role has been to sustain the body in the struggle against a powerful universe. A good camper knows that it is more important to be ingenious than to be a genius. And conversely, the body, by demonstrating the true meaning of sen-sual pleasure, has been of service to the mind. You feel the beauty of animal pleasure when you draw a deep breath of rich morning air right through your body, which has been carried by the cold night, curled up like an unborn child. How can you describe the feeling which wells up in the heart and stomach as the canoe finally rides up on the shore of the campsite after a long day of plunging your paddle into rain-swept waters? Purely physical is the joy which the fire spreads through the palms of your hands and the soles of your feet while your chattering mouth belches the poisonous cold. The pleasurable torpor of such a moment is perhaps not too different from what the mystics of the East are seeking. At least it has allowed me to taste what one respected gentleman used to call the joys of hard living.

Make no mistake, these joys are exclusively physical. They have nothing to do with the satisfaction of the mind when it imposes unwelcome work on the body, a satisfaction, moreover, which is often mixed with pride, and which the body never fails to avenge. During a very long and exhausting portage, I have sometimes felt my reason defeated, and shamefully fleeing, while my legs and shoulders carried bravely on. The mumbled verses which marked the rhythm of my steps at the beginning had become brutal grunts of "uh! uh! uh!" There was nothing aesthetic in that animal search for the bright clearing which always marks the end of a portage.

I do not want you to think that the mind is subjected to a healthy discipline merely by worrying about simplistic problems. I only wish to remind you of that principle of logic which states that valid conclusions do not generally follow from false premises. Now, in a canoe, where these premises are based on nature in its original state (rather than on books, ideas and habits of uncertain value), the mind conforms to that higher wisdom which we call natural philosophy; later, that healthy methodology and acquired humility will be useful in confronting mystical and spiritual questions.

I know a man whose school could never teach him patriotism, but who acquired that virtue when he felt in his bones the vastness of his land, and the greatness of those who founded it.

Canoeist, mouth of First Canyon, South Nahanni River, Northwest Territories. William D. Addison

Falls, Missinaibi River, Ontario. Ross B. Hodgetts

Morning sun reflected in beaver pond, Burleigh Game Preserve, Ontario. Bruce Litteljohn

Pitcher plant, Algonquin Provincial Park, Ontario. Ken Dudley

Reeds, Sturgeon Narrows, Quetico Provincial Park, Ontario. Bruce Litteljohn

Drowned trees, Eels' Creek, Kawartha Lakes, Ontario. Bruce Litteljohn

Sunset before storm, Thelon River, Northwest Territories. Dalton Muir

Burned forest, Kootenay National Park, British Columbia. Robert R. Taylor

FRED BODSWORTH

Wilderness Canada: Our Threatened Heritage

If we can agree that "wilderness" means any uninhabited region where the evidence of man's presence, past or current, is still relatively hidden, then Wilderness Canada is about 90% of our country—the greatest expanse of Great Outdoors outside Siberia.

We get indignant at foreigners who think that Canada is a vast backwoods inhabited mainly by moose, bear, Indians and Eskimoes. Canada, we protest, is one of the most urbanized and industrialized nations of the world, second highest in standard of living, fourth biggest exporter and all the rest. And we are right. But so are the foreigners. Canada, at least about 90% of it, *is* a vast backwoods inhabited mainly by moose, bear, Indians and Eskimoes.

Canada has spread its dominion from sea to sea, an east-west span of some 3,300 miles, but we have done it in the form of a narrow ribbon, in few places more than 200 miles wide, along our southern border, as though we were all afraid to get very far from the U.S.A. Canada has another dimension we often overlook. It stretches up there and spills off the top of the map in a spate of Arctic islands, the northernmost of them 2,800 miles north of Toronto or Montreal, to give our land a south-north dimension almost as great as our more familiar east-west span. If a Detroiter started travelling south and a neighbour across the border in Windsor started going north, and they matched mile for mile, the Detroiter would be sweating it out in the headwaters of the Amazon before the Windsorite stepped off the Canadian soil of Ellesmere Island onto the Arctic icecap. And almost all of the Windsorite's journey would be across uninhabited wilderness.

This is the measure of Wilderness Canada, a great northward-reaching solitude bigger than Australia, where the hand of man has touched lightly, and over immense distances has not touched at all.

We may contend that that great backwoods backyard is not the real Canada, yet the wilderness and all it symbolizes is probably a more diagnostic ingredient of Canada's social and economic identity than its cities, railways, highways and all the trappings of man. For if we consider our country as a whole, the Canadian land has shaped the spirit and nature of its people much more than Canadians, up to now, have reshaped their land. It is a fact that other people recognize more clearly than we do ourselves.

The fact of wilderness is imprinted deeply and intrinsically into almost every aspect of Canada's history. Wilderness waterways became the first routes of exploration, trade and colonization. Wilderness patterns determined the distribution of agricultural land suitable for settlement. The great pine forests of eastern Canada lured lumbermen who left behind them a denuded land but made it possible for tides of settlement to follow in their wake, some of it to prosper, some of it misguided and destined to languish and decay. The wilderness wealth of water power determined the sites of the first mills and communities, and later, in the form of electrical power, it selected the types of our modern industries and where they could locate.

Wilderness barriers still split Canada into four island-like pockets of development—from east to west, the Maritimes, the St. Lawrence Valley and Southern Ontario, the Prairies, and the Pacific Coast. Between these developed regions, confining them like battlements, are the wilderness barricades of Gaspé and Labrador, the rock-ribbed Canadian Shield of Northern Ontario, and the great ramparts of the Rockies. This wilderness fracturing of the country gives Canada a transportation overhead and problems of regionalism that no other nation of similarly modest population has had to overcome.

So the Canadian story is a dramatic interfusion of conquering wilderness where it could be conquered and adapting to it or bypassing it where conquest was defied. Above all, it selected Canadians and moulded the Canadian character, for those who could adjust to the wilderness fact and its harsh demands stayed to build a nation, and those who couldn't make the adjustment went elsewhere. Like all immigrant populations, Canadians have many origins, a diversity of cultures, but the fuel that fired the melting pot and gave us all a common, unifying heritage was the challenge and opportunities of a wilderness to be tamed. Every Canadian whose roots go back two generations or more, even though he may be a confirmed urbanite today, has the stamp of that wilderness selection impressed on his genes.

So Wilderness Canada, for all the naïve sentimentalizing that was once accorded it, nevertheless does have a deep and special meaning in the annals of Canadian nationhood. Our urbanizing world is going through a period of dreary standardization. To a growing extent, apartment high-rises, glassed-in skyscrapers, shopping plazas, expressways, traffic jams, even mechanized farms, are coming to look the same the world over. But one feature that makes Canada distinctive is the fact that no more than a hundred miles or so from every one of our cities lies a primeval wilderness frontier, a living link with our history that few other nations are privileged to have. The role of wilderness in our history, and its physical proximity, to this day still colour our character in subtle and unconscious ways. It is no coincidence that our national emblem is not a rising sun, a star, a hammer, a sickle or a dragon, but a beaver and a maple leaf. Nor is it coincidence that there are more paintings of wilderness lakes, spruce bogs and pine trees on more Canadian living-room walls than in any other nation on earth. We may scoff, we may deny, but the wilderness mystique is still a strong element of the Canadian ethos. And it is my belief that as urbanization continues in the future to fence us off from the natural world, our appreciation and need for wilderness will not dim, but will grow and assume a new form.

For wilderness values are changing. They are no longer fully or adequately measured in board feet, ore tonnages and kilowatts. The new value has dollar signs on it like the values of the past, but the dollar signs are receding and becoming harder to tally, because the new wilderness resource has ceased to be just grist for the mills of industry that can be measured, weighed or totalled on a corporation balance sheet. The new value is a subtle and abstract thing superficially labelled recreational potential. Wilderness has become a milieu in which the new urban man, surfeited with technological artificialities, can find and sink the biological roots of his wilderness ancestry, a balm and tonic for the intellect and soul. This is the new asset of Wilderness Canada—and the challenge.

For all the forbidding vastness of Canada's unsettled land, the new and changing scale of wilderness values is confronting Canada with a paradoxical wilderness crisis. We are in the incongruous situation of having some three million square miles of wilderness, yet we are rapidly running out of wilderness—the *kinds* of wilderness we need in the places we need it. For Wilderness Canada is not one wilderness; it is many wildernesses of many different types, and we have an embarrassing superabundance of some types but only a few disappearing tag ends of others.

We shall come back to modern man's need for wilderness, but first we must set down an inventory of the wildernesses of Wilderness Canada, what is happening to them, what we have lost and what we still have.

The most obvious indices of wilderness classification for the layman are trees and vegetation. In the popular mind, wilderness has come to mean forest, but this is an illogical restriction, because deserts, prairies and treeless tundra regions are wilderness as truly as forest regions. So our inventory of Wilderness Canada will be principally an examination of Canada's highly varied forest and vegetation zones.

Trees and plants do not grow at random; their distribution is sharply restricted by soil types and climate, and the principal climatic growth determiners are rainfall, mean summer temperatures, and length of growing season. Across a land as immense as Canada, conditions of soil and climate vary tremendously, and these variations have the effect of dividing the country's vegetation into zones which differ strikingly from one another.

The most significant and obvious divider is treeline, that northern boundary beyond which climatic conditions are too rigorous for trees to grow. North of it is treeless tundra, south of it is forest. Treeline, the barrier to the northward spread of forest, is not determined by any single, conveniently isolated factor; it is the result of a complex interplay of several factors, most of them climatic. A major control is the length of the summer growing season, established by the number of days each year over forty-three degrees Fahrenheit—the temperature at which plant cells can begin to reproduce and grow. Treeline lies roughly along the point where the growing season drops to under ninety days a year, for where the annual summer period is shorter than this, trees are usually incapable of producing sufficient growth to survive. However, treeline does not coincide precisely with the ninety-day growing season, for it is also influenced by regional variations in summer rainfall and by the frequency and dryness of winter winds.

Since climate is affected by the proximity of oceans, whether their coastal waters are warm or cold, and by the prevailing movements of air masses, treeline is not a neat east-west line established only by latitude. In Canada it is shaped strongly by three oceanic factors—the cold Labrador current of the Atlantic coast, the cold intrusion of Hudson Bay into the middle of the continent, and the warming effect that the Pacific's Japanese current has on the Yukon and northwest Arctic. Thus treeline starts in the east at the northern tip of Labrador and runs southwestward almost to James Bay, because of the icebox effect of Hudson Bay. From there it loops northwestward to reach the Arctic Ocean at the mouth of the Mackenzie River, because of the warmer climate that the Pacific bestows on British Columbia and the Yukon. The tundra region north of this line covers close to a million square miles, roughly half of it on the mainland and the other half on the Arctic islands. It represents a quarter of the total area of all Canada, and almost a third of the unsettled regions we are calling Wilderness Canada.

Tundra, though treeless, is far from plantless. It has a luxuriant vegetation of dwarfed flowering plants, lichens and mosses, which explode with green growth and brilliant bloom during the brief Arctic summer when the upper few inches of soil above the permafrost level thaws. Indeed it does have "trees" too, at least tree species, but they do not produce the sturdy upright growth of trees in more hospitable climes. There are several tundra-growing species of alders, birches and willows, but their woody stems hug the ground where the over-wintering buds are covered with snow and protected against the winter cold, the drying winds and the abrading blasts of snow. These stunted, creeping "trees" grow with extreme slowness but may live longer than many of the temperate zone trees we know. An Arctic willow may have 100 annual growth rings packed into a woody stem the size of a lead pencil; occasionally one with a "trunk" an inch in diameter will be 400 years old.

At treeline the tundra merges with the vast belt of coniferous woodland that foresters call boreal forest or taiga. This is far and away our most widespread forest region, covering more than half of Canada. It sweeps in a great arc with a north-south depth of 500 to 600 miles from Newfoundland and Labrador across Quebec, Northern Ontario, the Northern Prairie Provinces, to the eastern foothills of the Rockies and northwestward to the Yukon and Alaska.

The boreal forest region is composed mainly of coniferous, needle-leafed trees—spruce, balsam fir, tamarack and jack pine—because these evergreen species are best adapted to grow in regions where the growing season is short and the winters long, cold and dry. They are able to retain their needle-like leaves over winter because leaves of this type, with tough, resinous coatings and little surface exposure, resist low temperatures and evaporation of their water to the dry winter cold. The latter—resistance to winter water loss through leaf evaporation—is the most essential requirement for tree growth in this subarctic region. And since evergreen trees don't have to produce a new crop of leaves every spring, they survive a short growing season by being ready to begin food production and growth as soon as spring temperatures become suitable.

When we say "north woods," this is the forest zone we mean. Its coniferous trees, slender, conical, spire-like, present a very different aspect from the spreading, spherical, deciduous trees of forests farther south—a skyline that looks like a jagged picket fence instead of an undulating roller coaster.

All of the boreal forest region except its western flank along the Rockies coincides closely with the Canadian Shield, the massive horseshoe of ancient Precambrian rock which loops around Hudson Bay, and for this reason it has a distinctive geological character as well as being a homogeneous forest region. The Canadian Shield is a segment of the earth's original crust which first cooled three billion years ago; it is our planet's largest mass of surface-exposed Precambrian rock, for in most regions of the world it is buried deeply by rock strata of more recent volcanic and sedimentary origin.

Since the Shield is an ancient worn-down mountain range, much of it is rolling country with the roots of its mountains still showing through. It is a land pocked with hundreds of thousands of lake basins and peat-filled bogs, and trenched with a labyrinth of rivers that are punctuated with white falls and tossing rapids because of the abrupt changes in the land's elevations. It is thinly soiled, its bald knobs of grey, banded rock exposed throughout much of its area, for whatever soil may have been there in an earlier era was planed away and carried southward by the Ice Age glaciers that crept back across this northern land for the last time only 8,000 years ago.

The Shield is a treasure house of minerals that has contributed more raw materials to the development of Canada's modern industrial economy than all the rest of the country combined. And the boreal forest it supports provides almost all Canada's pulpwood and paper, our leading export and dollar-earner.

The southern boundary of the boreal forest is a line where the growing season extends to around 150 days, as against treeline's ninety days. The 150-day line snakes across Canada from the Maritimes through Southern Quebec and Central Ontario, and makes a northward loop around the Prairies. South of this line, deciduous trees—trees that can afford the biological affluence of shedding foliage every autumn and producing new foliage every spring—can grow.

With the two regions—tundra and boreal forest—we have accounted for almost 3,000,000 square miles of Canada, more than three-quarters of our land, and virtually all of Wilderness Canada. But in the primeval Canada, the Canada that was *all* wilderness, there were several other smaller regions which represented northern extensions of forest and grassland zones that had their main areas south of Canada. These smaller vegetation zones that lie south and, in the British Columbia mountain area, west of the boreal forest region, are the zones that have been altered most by the settlement, agriculture and industry of man. They are products of variations in rainfall more than in length of growing season, and, since Canada's rainfall story begins with moisture-laden winds off the Pacific, we shall wind up our wilderness inventory by tracing the rainfall pattern from west to east across Canada and by examining the profound effect it has on vegetation.

Air masses saturated with moisture from having moved across thousands of miles of warm Pacific are piled up against the towering barrier of British Columbia's Coast Mountains by the prevailing westerly winds. Deflected upward by the mountains, the air cools, its water-holding capacity drops, and the excess moisture it can no longer carry is dumped out as rain. This gives the western coastal strip of Canada one of the highest rainfalls of the world, averaging more than 100 inches a year, and soaring to more than 300 inches in some pockets.

This tremendous rainfall and the balmy year-round climate that goes with it have produced a highly specialized coastal rain forest characterized by gigantic trees and a lush, dense undergrowth of mosses, ferns and shrubs. Abundant moisture and a growing season that lasts most of the year permit trees like Douglas fir, western red cedars, western hemlocks and Sitka spruce to grow to 300 feet in height and attain venerable ages of 1,500 years. Some of these trees started growth when the Roman Empire was still flourishing. The coastal rain forest is the smallest distinctive forest region of Canada, but in the few pockets where some of its patriarchs and giants still survive, it is the most awesome and spectacular segment of Wilderness Canada.

When the saturated air mass off the Pacific spills over the top of the Coast Mountains and begins sinking down the eastern slopes, it becomes warmer air again, capable of holding its moisture, and rainfall suddenly decreases. As a result, the forest abruptly changes. The mountain forests of British Columbia's interior form an interwoven montage of three forest regions—Montane on the dry eastern mountain slopes, Columbia on the wet western slopes, and Subalpine at high altitudes. They are mostly coniferous trees, species such as Engelmann spruce and ponderosa and lodgepole pines which grow nowhere in Canada except in this mountain region, and they are incapable of attaining the great size of the coast forest giants.

British Columbia is a series of north-south mountain ranges, so the eastward-flowing Pacific air is bumped up and down like a roller coaster. At each rise up a western-facing mountain slope it has to dump out more of its moisture; at each drop down an eastern slope it clings to whatever moisture it still retains. After several ups and downs of this kind, when it finally drops down the east side of the Rockies to the Prairies, it is wrung relatively dry. The air that drenches the coastal forest with 100 inches or more of rain per year deposits only ten to twenty inches a year on the Prairies.

The reasons the Prairies are treeless, like the reasons for the existence of the treeline, are a combination of interacting factors, but the basic one is low rainfall. Trees are weak competitors for growing space under such arid conditions. Grasses, on the other hand, with their short, rapid cycles of growth and their ability to withstand periods of drought, can grow lushly where rainfall is as limited as ten inches a year. Thus, in the struggle between grasses and trees for possession of the western plains when the glaciers moved back 8,000 years ago, the grasses won and they still hold the trees at bay.

Rainfall increases slowly as one continues eastward into the range of storms bearing moisture from the Great Lakes, the Gulf of Mexico and the Atlantic. From a low of under fifteen inches a year in the Alberta prairies, it rises to twenty inches in Southern Manitoba, thirty in Southern Ontario, forty-two at Montreal and fifty-five in the Maritimes. At the Manitoba-Ontario boundary annual rainfall reaches twenty-five inches and this tips the balance in favour of trees over grasses; the grassland ends, and forest takes over again.

The remaining region of Eastern Canada is an area of longer growing seasons and increased rainfall, compared to the coniferous boreal forest to the north of it, and this permits deciduous trees to become major forest components. This region includes a section of Northwestern Ontario from the Manitoba border to Lake Superior, all of Central and Southern Ontario, the St. Lawrence Valley and the Maritimes. Foresters split it up into three different regional forest types, but for our purpose we can lump it all together and call it the eastern deciduous woodland. Characteristic deciduous trees here are the maples, yellow birch, beech, oaks, ashes and several others.

There is no sharp line separating it from the boreal forest to the north. Instead, there is a broad transitional zone where boreal spruces and balsam fir are mixed with deciduous species, the northern conifers gradually becoming rarer and the deciduous species more abundant as one progresses southward. Most of the Maritimes is in this transitional zone with conifers more abundant than deciduous hardwoods, giving the forests of the Maritimes a strong boreal forest character.

In Canada, the deciduous hardwoods really come into their own only in the St. Lawrence Valley and in Southern Ontario from the region of Algonquin Park southward, where they represent northern extensions of the main North American deciduous forest which originally covered all of the eastern United States. In fact, in its purest form, it exists only in deep Southwestern Ontario south of a line from around Toronto to the south end of Lake Huron. This strip along the north shore of Lake Erie, known to foresters and botanists as the Carolinian Zone, has an exotic character, for it contains a number of southern tree species such as chestnut, hickory, sycamore, tulip tree, honey locust, sassafras and Kentucky coffee tree that grow nowhere else in Canada.

So this was the varied tapestry of Wilderness Canada before the heavy hand of man fell upon it. How has it fared? And what is happening to it today?

When the first settlers pushed up the St. Lawrence Valley into what is now Southern Ontario, they were confronted with a 50,000-square-mile tract of mainly deciduous forest so dense that a squirrel could have travelled from the St. Lawrence to the Detroit River without touching the ground. Today virtually all of this has been cleared and settled by man, or allowed to grow back into second-growth forest that is logged whenever trees reach a marketable size. Of that original 50,000 square miles of hardwoods, only a few thousand acres now in parks or Conservation Authority forests have managed to escape the axe and saw and remain in anything like their primeval condition. The chestnut is gone, probably forever, victim of a blight brought in by man; the elm is going from a similar cause. Also gone, at least in their original majestic form, are the pure stands of white pines which once interspersed this hardwood zone to form eastern North America's most impressive forest type, rivalling the great, cathedral-like fir and cedar forests of the Pacific Coast. The few pathetic remnants of Southern Ontario's primitive hardwood forest that survive today are precious, living, outdoor museums, and their great, tightly-packed groves of maples, birches and oaks tell us far more about pioneer courage and endurance than do museums filled with spinning wheels and flintlock muskets.

Another major division of Wilderness Canada that has been almost completely occupied and altered by man is the prairie grass-land of the West. Adapted by nature for the growth of grasses, it was of course ideal territory for the production of man's domesticated grasses—the grain crops that are the mainstay of modern man's food supply. Very little of it has escaped drainage and the plough. There are only tiny remnants of undisturbed prairie where the native flora still survive—scattered islands of the original grassland wilderness hemmed in now by a vast, monotonous sea of the alien crops of man.

Across the mountains, that other highly distinctive piece of Wilderness Canada, the coastal rain forest, is also largely gone. The towering Douglas firs and cedars were, and still are, the most valuable lumbering trees in Canada. Their tendencies to concentrate in lowlands near the sea put the most commercially valuable stands where they were readily accessible to loggers. As a result, practically all the primeval rain forest is gone today except for a few tag ends in parks and reserves, and in out-of-the-way valleys that loggers have not yet reached. There are many examples of big trees still standing, such as those in Vancouver's Stanley Park, but most such survivors stand alone or in small groups, isolated sample copies, no longer in their genuine rain-forest setting. The finest and most accessible example of a rain forest that has been preserved intact is Cathedral Grove on Vancouver Island's Alberni Highway. Here a couple of hundred acres of 800-year-old Douglas firs tower higher than twenty-storey buildings and represent one of the most impressive remnants of virgin Canada that we have. Cathedral Grove deserves to be known as well as Niagara Falls, for it is a natural wonder of equal calibre.

Two remaining southern forest regions, the British Columbia interior and the Maritimes, have pockets of uninhabited territory, but their wilderness fabric has become tattered and threadbare with the spreading roads, towns, mines and logging activities of man. So our quest for really extensive tracts of unspoiled Wilderness Canada is left with the two great northern regions—the boreal forest or taiga and the Arctic tundra. However, this is not exactly backing us into a tight, little corner, for, as we have seen earlier, these two regions span 3,000,000 square miles and cover more than three-quarters of Canada.

This is the immense heartland of Wilderness Canada. Its southern periphery is pierced here and there by roads and railways, and it is dotted thinly with small towns, trading posts, mines and military establishments. But the land is vast, the works of man dispersed like ships at sea, and by even the purest definition most of it is still wilderness.

There has been a traditional belief throughout Canada's history that this huge, rocky and boggy northland can never be significantly occupied or changed by man. Today that old Canadian cliché is beginning to appear in doubt. It is probably true that the boreal forest and Arctic tundra regions will never be populated to any significant extent, but today's technological, machine-powered man no longer has to move into a region and live there permanently in large numbers to change and despoil the face of a land. Small crews with modern machinery can do what armies could not do in the past.

A single big hydroelectric dam may itself be only a pinpoint on the map, but it can raise the levels of streams and lakes throughout a vast region behind it, flooding hundreds of miles of shoreline, drowning forests and turning those shorelines into an impenetrable tangle of dead, still-standing trees that will destroy whole watersheds for fishing, boating and canoeing for generations to come. Numerous scenic lakes throughout the north have been transformed into ugly, muddy reservoirs in this manner without a man or a bulldozer coming within a hundred miles of them.

A pulp mill may occupy only a few hundred yards of a river's frontage, but its pollution can destroy the river for a hundred miles downstream.

DDT sprayed over a few square miles of forest can be carried by streams, and can poison waterways scores of miles away.

Sulphur fumes from a single smelter smokestack can kill all vegetation and turn hundreds of square miles downwind into a barren, rocky desert.

Loggers may occupy a forest region for only a few months or a year, but if they have not followed proper logging methods they leave behind a terrain in which mountain slopes are gouged with landslides, soil eroded, humus burned by ground-slash fires, and the region is doomed to remain a scrubby wasteland for a century.

The new threat to the Arctic wilderness is the discovery of oil, and the forecasts that it may become a gigantic oil field richer than Kuwait. Exploration crews are ranging across the Arctic landscape, their tractor-trains ripping up the thin tundra soil. Behind them, inevitably, they leave a litter of drilling equipment, because Arctic transportation costs are so high it is usually more economic to abandon used equipment than freight it out again. Oil fields mean accidents, leaks and pollution of the filthiest and most persistent kind. They also entail maintenance roads and pipelines snaking across hundreds of miles of virgin terrain, and pipelines become barriers to the movement of wildlife, blocking seasonal migrations that mammals like caribou must make in order to survive.

So man doesn't have to move in and settle down to destroy wilderness. He is now capable of a destruction out of all proportion to the size of the resident population causing it.

Wilderness has its physical elements—forest, clean water, space, virgin flora and wildlife, but its essence is none of these. Essentially wilderness is an abstract, intangible thing—an impression, a mood, an illusion of solitude and remoteness, of having shucked off and left far behind the shams and sophistries of man's artificial world. And since it is a "feel" rather than a "thing," it can be marred, or its impact drastically diluted, with relatively little acute destruction of its physical elements. A forest may still stand and a rapids may still roar, but the distant rumble of a power saw, a logging truck or a float plane landing on a remote lake can shatter in an instant the wilderness traveller's illusion of having cut himself off from other men.

Thus, wilderness is fragile, its evanescent qualities highly vulnerable to the long, outreaching tentacles of modern, resource-hungry, technological man. We can only destroy it; we can't bring it back.

In this light, even the enormous Arctic and subarctic reaches of Wilderness Canada are not immune to dilution and destruction. More and more, they are being pocked and gouged by the inroads of man in his endless scouring of the earth for its timber, ores and oil. Our tundra and boreal forest regions will never be thickly populated or completely erased for farmland and urban developments as the deciduous wilderness of Southern Ontario has been. But man now has the power and incentive to riddle the north with dams, transmission lines, roads, pipelines and landing strips which can reach out and creep together until even this last great bastion of Wilderness Canada is cut up into pieces so small that its wilderness character will disappear.

Will it matter? Or should we chalk it up as another proud victory in man's self-delegated, exploitive mission to revamp the whole surface of the earth in the name of human progress?

I believe it *will* matter. I am not blind to the fact that tapping the earth for its natural resources produces creature comforts I am grateful to have; I like my central heating, my hot shower, my car, and the system that provides me with California oranges in January, as much as the next man. But if maintaining that system into the future requires transforming our planet into a human ant hill from which all vestiges of the natural, primeval world are to be slowly obliterated, we shall be depriving ourselves of other values as essential as the resource-based creature comforts we have gained. For man needs contact with wilderness and wild nature as much as he needs the foodstuffs, ores and fuels that a tamed nature can yield. And perhaps Canadians, with that stamp of wilderness selection on their ancestry and their genes, need wilderness a little more than other peoples whose struggle against a virgin land belongs to an earlier, forgotten stage of their histories. But I suggest that national distinction for Canadians with somewhat limited conviction. All mankind, not just Canadians, is still so close to the wilderness stage of our history, in terms of the genetic and evolutionary time scale, that national differences of a few centuries are of little significance.

Science needs wilderness and samples of virgin land of all kinds, because the only way science can accurately measure the impact of man's varied activities on land is to have undisturbed control areas with which to make comparisons.

Industry needs it for the renewable resources, especially timber, that a healthy wilderness will produce in perpetuity.

Perhaps we need it more than we yet know as a climatic control and as a replenisher and circulator of the atmosphere's moisture and oxygen.

But above all, in this crowded age, man needs wilderness more than ever before as a place to find ancestral roots, to look back and see where he has been; he needs it as a psychological safety valve for all the smothered, pent-up, artificially-induced tensions and frustrations of a way of life that he is not yet fully adapted to live. Call it recreation, but it involves much more than just having fun.

Man as a species had evolved into something near his present form 2,000,000 years ago. Throughout 99.5% of his history, he remained a nomadic hunter and fisherman, simply another predator like the wolf and the lion, living as part of the natural order. About 10,000 years ago, he began to short-cut the food-getting process by the development of agriculture, but as a herdsman, sower and harvester he still retained a pastoral life close to nature and the soil. Towns and cities began to appear a few thousand years ago, but it was only with the industrial revolution which began two centuries ago that large numbers of men could lead lives completely divorced from nature and natural processes. In fact, it has been only in the past few decades that giant metropolises have developed and urban life has become the lot of most of mankind.

So the modern city is only moments old in terms of the evolutionary time scale that moulded man's basic nature. The crowded, regimented, fast-paced, urban life that most humans lead today is an extreme and highly unnatural distortion of the life that man has led throughout virtually all his past. It is so recent that we are still ignorant of its long-term effects on human nature and health, but urban crime, violence, suicide rates, mental disease rates and a number of other such indicators are stressing graphically that man is having serious problems adapting to the new urban life he has chosen.

Basic animal natures alter slowly. Adaptations to a new environment come in the form of gradual changes spread out over many generations—be they mice, hummingbirds or men. Maybe some day man will be a thoroughly urbanized creature happily adapted to a life hemmed in by bricks, concrete and hordes of other men, but he is not that kind of creature yet. He still bears the imprint, the genetic nostalgia, of a species whose life for 2,000,000 years has been regulated by the changing seasons, the sunsets, the rain—in short, by wilderness, that segment of the environment outside the realm of man.

I suggest that many commonplace features of modern living are in their essence expressions of urban man's wilderness nostalgia—the move to suburbia for its bit of green space and blue sky, summer cottages, flower gardens, geraniums on a window sill, the keeping of pets, the wilderness paintings on our walls, and the log fires in our fireplaces. In their subtle way, they are all a harking back to a wilderness past we may have forgotten consciously but which is still there thinly veiled in the subconscious.

But the most obvious expressions of that wilderness nostalgia is the camping explosion that has been a world-wide phenomenon of the past decade or two. This is a direct and simple seeking of wilderness in a form that leaves no scope for misinterpretation. As soon as urbanites acquired some mobility and leisure, what did they do with it? Thousands of them headed for the nearest wilderness. And in the case of Canada, the realization was suddenly driven home that we had pushed back the frontier too far and were short of wilderness areas in regions near population centres where it was needed now for recreational use. Which takes us back to the statement made early in this chapter that, despite the vastness of Wilderness Canada, our country faces a wilderness crisis—a shortage of the kinds of wilderness we need in the places where we need it.

The participants in this mass return to nature vary widely in the depth and intensity of the wilderness experience they seek. A majority are satisfied with the sort of wilderness-at-a-distance experience they can obtain at a crowded, public campground or at a lakeside tourist lodge, but even for them an essential part of the lure is that there be real wilderness just across the lake or over the hill. But a rapidly swelling segment of them are connoisseurs who want their wilderness experience pure. They don't just want to touch the fraying hem of wilderness, they want to cloak themselves in the whole garment. They want to get *into* wilderness country deeply enough to shed all the cares and reminders of the workaday world that has them enslaved at all other times. They have discovered that the surest and most thorough way of escaping modern life's pressures is to return, if only briefly, to the simple, unpretentious life their forebears led before all the modern pressures evolved. And this context channels us into a somewhat more restricted definition of wilderness than the broad concept of virgin territory that we have previously been considering, because to qualify wilderness as "escape" it has to be a region that can be conveniently reached from the population centres where its users live, and it has to be capable of being travelled when the users get there.

Most wilderness buffs shun mechanical aids to travel, such as outboards and snowmobiles, as destroyers of the wilderness solitude they are seeking. Hiking, of course, qualifies as an acceptable mode of wilderness travel, but it places stringent limitations on that magic lure of putting the miles behind one. "Escape" wilderness, in the Canadian context, almost by definition demands areas with lake and river chains and short portages for canoe travel, or, in the West, areas with trails and mountain pastures that permit the use of packhorses. Canoes and horses are the only practical conveyances that will carry the camping outfit required for a long trip without destroying wilderness qualities.

Very little of Wilderness Canada is canoeing or packhorse country within a one-day drive of major cities. The far north is laced with canoe routes, but most of them are hazardous, suitable only for the hardy and experienced, and in any case the logistic problems of getting canoes and camping gear into them put them out of bounds for the average canoe-tripping vacationist who wants to drive no more than a day, launch his canoe and take off for the wilderness. As a result, accessible canoe country such as Ontario's Algonquin Park is so crowded with voyageurs during vacation seasons that the wilderness illusion is shattered by the flotillas of wilderness seekers.

So our survey of Wilderness Canada began in broad terms with a picture of wilderness in abundance. But when we reduce it to the more meaningful terms of wilderness that can be conveniently reached and used by man, the abundance shrinks to scarcity.

Recreational wilderness has become a precious asset. It is a dynamic element of our historical heritage and we need it as living museums where men can see and experience the primitive Canada that was. We need it as meccas of pilgrimage into our species' past, as sanctuaries of reorientation where we can reduce life to the essentials of food and shelter, and in this clearer, untrammelled view see ourselves as part of the system of nature, not demigods above or outside it.

We have recognized for a long time that wildlife needs sanctuaries to protect it against the habitat destruction wrought by man. But man in modern times is wreaking a violent destruction on his own primitive habitat, the habitat that moulded him into the species he is, and we are beginning to recognize that wilderness regions have cultural and recreational values that make them sanctuaries for humans.

Wilderness Canada is indeed vast. But its vastness gives a false picture. Those wilderness segments that fill the requirements of sanctuaries for man are in short supply and still shrinking. Wilderness shaped our past, but it will have even greater importance as an antidote to the perils of urban crowding and synthesized living in the future. In our polluted, uglifying world, the Wilderness Canada that remains has become an inheritance to be preserved and cherished.

Thelon River, Northwest Territories. Dalton Muir

31

Wilberforce Falls, Hood River, Northwest Territories. William I. Campbell

Moss, Burleigh Game Preserve, Ontario. Bruce Litteljohn

Reeds, Wasaks Lake, Timagami region, Ontario. Wayland Drew

Sunrise, Kaogassikok (Pickerel) Lake, Rainy River District, Ontario. Bruce Litteljohn

Sunrise, Crow River, Algonquin Provincial Park, Ontario. John G. Foster

Sand cherries, October, Georgian Bay, Ontario. William D. Addison

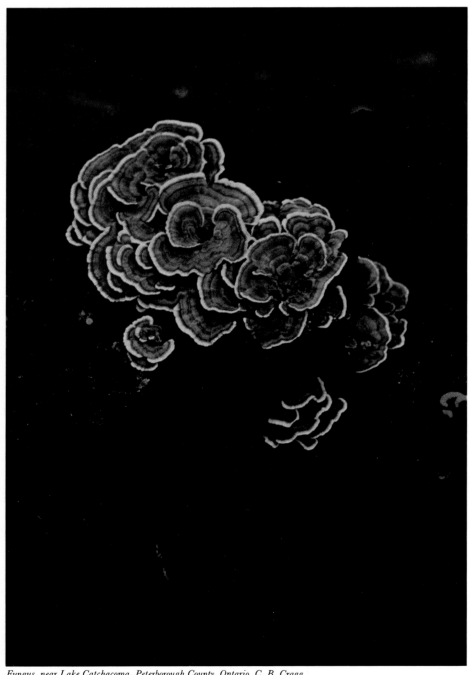

Fungus, near Lake Catchacoma, Peterborough County, Ontario. C. B. Cragg

Birch and aspen, near Sioux Narrows, Ontario. Robert R. Taylor

39

Kaskawulsh Glacier, Kluane Lake, Yukon Territory. Dalton Muir–National Parks

40

Edge of Steele Glacier, near Kluane Lake, Yukon Territory. Dalton Muir–National Parks

Winter shoreline, Stoney Lake, Kawartha region, Ontario. Bruce Litteljohn

Steele Glacier, Yukon Territory. Dalton Muir–National Parks

Stacks Rapids, Petawawa River, Algonquin Provincial Park, Ontario. William C. Mason

45

Moraine Creek Valley, Alberta. Robert R. Taylor

47

Terminal moraine in snow, Moraine Lake, Alberta. Robert R. Taylor

ERIC W. MORSE

Challenge and Response: The Modern Voyageur

For centuries, man has devoted most of his effort to making life more comfortable and secure—until every so often it becomes *uncomfortably* secure. There comes an urge for escape into a world where there is some risk. No one would wish to set the clock back and revert to hardship and adventure as a permanent way of life. But civilized living in a modern city lacks zest. Much of Canada, especially that part "north of sixty," lies ready to supply the adventurer with what he needs temporarily to balance his existence. The wilderness traveller relishes variety and revels in keeping going, by whatever vehicle the terrain and season dictate. In Canada, he can keep going for a long time, as hundreds of thousands of square miles of wilderness still lie open to him—on mountain, along seacoast, or in forest-lakeland. This wilderness is not always pretty, not everywhere grand; it contains swamps, has areas of burnt-over misery, lies for a million square miles in Arctic Barren Lands; and its temperatures range through 150 degrees. Wilderness travel is therefore a challenge.

The nature of the challenge can be conveyed better perhaps by recounting specific trips than by discussion of principles. In fifty years of such travel, I look back on four particular journeys as providing different kinds of challenge. It happens that all were by canoe. The canoe uniquely meets Canadian conditions. With half the freshwater surface of the world in Canada, and with a craft not only capable of carrying sufficient supplies, but capable itself of being carried comfortably by one person past the many navigational obstacles, the canoe permits the *deepest penetration* of wilderness. With today's freeze-dried foods, a canoe party can travel for four weeks, a distance of six or seven hundred miles, without needing to touch at a reprovisioning post, and still stay within the sensible limit of 100 pounds total equipment per man. Food-drops at prearranged sites permit two or three times this range. A kayak is faster on flat water and can navigate boiling rapids, but it is very limited in carrying capacity, and awkward to portage. A horse can carry much more than a man, but it needs to be fed—as does a dog team. This either limits the terrain in which these can move, or adds to the load. The canoe, it is true, is restricted to water, but in Canada this is not a serious limitation, except in mountains.

The first trip I would record was by canoe from Fort William to Sault Ste. Marie, 400 miles around Lake Superior's north shore. An important ingredient of the challenge, it turned out, was no more than meeting the unknown. Superior is an inland sea which, because of its great depth, never really warms up, so the large areas of hot, bare rock around it set up violent air currents and squalls. In a few short stretches of up to ten miles the shores are rocky precipices rising 500 feet from the water. It did not take us long to discover, however, that the waves on such a deep lake, though big, were long. We could paddle in six-foot waves that came from astern, or four-foot waves on our beam. Squalls hit hard and suddenly, but came only with certain atmospheric conditions; in any case for 100 of the 400 miles there was a screen of islands along the coast, and little harbours everywhere. In making traverses across the mouths of bays—some up to forty or fifty miles deep—we made sure we stayed on a course that kept us within four miles (an hour's paddle) of at least an island for refuge. When it became too rough, we just put ashore and waited. It worked out that one could move on an average two days in three. Our only serious gamble was a straight-south run of twenty miles with a rocky wall to the east and a single available landfall midway, where the object was to get out of Michipicoten Bay. We rose at four a.m., were on the water at six, and made the twenty miles in four hours, scudding before a strong north wind and hissing waves. Only half an hour after we reached our objective, a squall struck—but we were then conveniently close to an island offering a safe takeout.

Lake Superior is a good example of the fact that, even in our day, sections of unspoiled and scenic wilderness are to be found where conditions are too difficult or too dangerous for family vacations, fishing parties or the "beer-can brigade." There is still plenty of primitive wilderness available for those who are prepared to cope with the protecting factors, whether they be wind, waves, insects or inaccessibility.

Different wilderness challenges evoke special psychological qualities: patience, stubbornness, boldness or just dumb brute force. A trip requiring plenty of the latter is an old fur-traders' and (later) Klondikers' route passing from the delta of the Mackenzie River up the Rat River, over McDougall Pass through the starkly beautiful Richardson Mountains, and down the Bell and Porcupine Rivers to the Yukon River at Fort Yukon in Alaska. Actually this pass (at a little over 1,000 feet altitude) is by far the lowest one on the whole continental spine from below the U.S. border to the Arctic Sea. But the thousand feet must be achieved in forty-five miles. While only half a mile of actual portaging at the summit separates the two great basins of the Mackenzie and the Yukon, no one should undertake the upward part of this canoe trip under the illusion that it can be paddled. About nine days of toil, averaging only five miles progress a day, are required; one wades or poles or drags the canoe up miles of virtually continuous, shallow rapids. The mountain scenery rising 4,000 feet above the pass alone is worth this journey. The westward course down, by contrast, is almost boringly easy—at fifty and sixty miles a day in the fast current.

In a series of trips going from Hudson Bay to Alaska in the general latitude of the Arctic Circle, I recall our first Barren Lands journey, in 1962, as the one when we were most keenly aware of challenge. It was not the trip itself, for the Hanbury and Thelon Rivers make perhaps the safest and easiest of the trips in this area. It was again, as on Lake Superior, no more than facing the unknown. The continental part of the Barren Lands is a vast no-man's-land lying between Indians south of the treeline and Eskimoes living along the seacoast. If an accident occurred in this rugged country of high winds and short summers, of dense insect population and no people, it would be different from a mishap near home. We knew that this austere and unrelenting land rarely gives a second chance. Our party of four were, I believe, among the first *tourists* to canoe across this area. Those who had gone before us were mappers, trappers, prospectors or wildlife personnel, who were supported by government or commerce. When our charter plane dropped us and flew off, we were on our own, and sensed high adventure. This is one of the world's few remaining large areas of virgin wilderness, with plenty of big game. We found that the insects had been grossly overrated—not in their numbers but in their effectiveness in the almost ever-present high wind. The wind, however, later turned out to be a problem, for we were pinned down completely for five days, and in another five achieved barely forty miles. Nevertheless, rested if nothing else, and with the benefit of continuous daylight, we put on a marathon effort when the wind let up, and were able to make our rendezvous with the returning plane. We managed to overcome new conditions: absence of firewood for many miles; the insects on cloudy, still days; the polar gales; the icy water in big lakes. The unknown factor had merely added spice.

Of wilderness trips I have taken, I would pick above all others—both for its challenge and for its rewards—the descent of the Coppermine River, from Lac de Gras, near its source, down 400 miles to Coronation Gulf on the Arctic Sea. This river starts in the Barrens; but sparse spruce woods floor its valley from Point Lake to within thirty miles of the sea. The chief challenge that the Coppermine offers is its rapids. In its upper reaches these are shallow and rocky; then, following a series of long lakes, the rapids occur in gradually deepening canyons. One of these, named the Rocky Defile by Franklin, has 150-foot walls. In its lower reaches, approaching the sea, the Coppermine has sections where it drops at eighteen feet to the mile, which is about the limit of safety for undecked canoes. In some of the canyons are series of transverse dikes of harder rock with gaps occurring, for added excitement, now on one side of the river, now on the other. The canyons can be portaged past, of course, but only through tangled willows up a game trail and then steeply down. A nice balance of boldness and caution was called for, plus special techniques and equipment. In the end we found it necessary to portage a total of only six or seven of the 400 miles, and to "line" the canoe here and there. Again, the formidable navigational problems had served as protectors of wilderness; this was not country for power boats. A principal reward was the game: paddling through a herd of swimming caribou, or having caribou graze through our camp as though it were a barnyard; wolverines; many white wolves, some circling curiously to scent the strange intruders; a considerable number of moose which had moved quite recently into the area. On other Barrens trips nearby, we had seen grizzly and musk oxen.

These four specific trips—Lake Superior, the Rat-Porcupine, our first Barren Lands trip, and the Coppermine—are selected, not for pulp-magazine content, but as representative challenges and to illustrate how difficulties and danger can be safely met. Most of the danger in wilderness travel is avoidable by anticipating it. It is a little like the case of a husband with an explosive temper who beats his wife without provocation: in time she learns when to tiptoe past, and when to hide. It is not that this lake or that river can *never* be travelled; but a matter of recognizing a dangerous mood or of avoiding a dangerous section. The dangers arise from poor briefing, bad judgement, bravado and picking wrong equipment or crew. Examples abound: in 1966 on the Coppermine above the Arctic Circle we rescued from drowning a couple who upset in a rapid with too small a craft (and only a week's supply of food for a fortnight's trip). In the early 1950's two different two-man parties set off for northern wilderness trips with but a single canoe; no trace of either has since been found. The cause of these tragedies may never be known—except that there was no accompanying canoe to rescue them. In 1967, allegedly experienced canoeists set off down the Back River on the Barrens with all their baggage and *three* to an eighteen-foot canoe, which predictably foundered in a rapid. Two perished. The files of the R.C.M.P. are full of such cases. Nevertheless, the fact is that there is no country in the world with wilderness so vast as Canada's, yet—in the absence of hostile tribes, lethal insects, dangerous wild animals and (virtually) of poisonous snakes—so *safe* for travel, for those who will learn its ways.

The Canadian wilderness travellers *par excellence* were the *coureurs de bois* and the voyageurs of fur-trade days. In an age before road or rail, thousands of tons of furs were annually brought out to the sea from as far away as the Rockies and the Mackenzie, and thousands of tons of manufactured trade goods taken back, transported by rivers and lakes. One main route led from Montreal, up the Ottawa River, across to the French, around the north shores of Lakes Huron and Superior, thence steeply up to the divide and down westward-flowing tributaries into Lake Winnipeg. Another route led into the northern end of Lake Winnipeg from York Factory at the mouth of the Hayes and Nelson. Westward from Lake Winnipeg, the Saskatchewan River led the fur traders either to Edmonton, or passing to the Churchill River and over another continental divide down to the Athabasca. The great northern *entrepôt*, the end of the line, was Fort Chipewyan on Lake Athabasca. Even west and north of here, subsidiary trade routes went up the Peace or the Liard and down the Mackenzie or Yukon, or passed inland from the Columbia; so that after the Hudson's Bay Company in 1821 had absorbed the Northwest Company, its empire covered virtually all of continental Canada.

Most of these rugged water routes lie today practically unchanged from what the first fur-seekers saw. In these areas the original portages, in use for centuries, are still, in fact, the only means of overcoming local navigational obstacles. For added drama, in areas preserved from logging, the portages are shaded by tall pines which could have been seedlings when the first explorers passed.

One cannot fail to be impressed by the toughness of the early voyageurs. Though there were also Indians and Orkneymen, perhaps the most colourful and celebrated voyageurs were the *Canadiens*. Their life on the trail, extending for six or eight weeks at a stretch, was a killing one—literally so, for the early journals speak of clusters of crude crosses marking graves at many a particularly dangerous rapid. Being roused at two or three a.m., off before breakfast, paddling up to fifty and sixty strokes to the minute (except for an hourly *pipe*), and continuing this pace for a sixteen-hour day—such things were simply taken for granted. Over each portage a voyageur was responsible for carrying half a dozen ninety-pound packs, usually in three 180-pound loads.

The voyageurs' diet was not a lush one. Beans, peas, maize—prototypes of modern dehydrated foods—were the staples for Lake Superior and east. On the Prairies and to the northwest the diet rarely varied from pemmican.

One of the most impressive aspects of the fur-trade era was how the fur companies—the Montrealers in particular—organized the logistics, when only primitive transportation was available. From the Indian birchbark canoe they developed a bark freight canoe nearly forty feet long. To overcome the vast distance within the limited time from break-up to freeze-up, the fur canoes started off nearly simultaneously in early May from opposite ends of the main line, met at a great depot, Grand Portage (later at Fort William) on Lake Superior, and exchanged cargoes. The fur trade was critically important in extending and establishing Canada's boundaries and in providing the economic spinal cord of an independent northern nation.

A growing number of Canadians including, gratifyingly, many younger ones, have found a rewarding way to combine adventure with history and physical fitness in a holiday spent in retracing by canoe a stretch of one or another of these old fur-trade highways. The past comes up vividly, and in three dimensions. This story is the very bone and marrow of Canada.

The requirements for modern wilderness travel are basically three. First is *equipment;* here one's needs should be established by the most thorough briefing. The prime need is to select the right vehicle. The canoe for a quiet moonlight paddle can be very different in size and material from what is required for a trip in the north, where a seventeen-or-eighteen-foot aluminum or fiberglass canoe, built to carry 600 pounds and still allow eight inches' freeboard, is essential. Accessory equipment is equally important. On the Rat we took dry-suit lowers to wear over wool, which spared us swollen legs while wading in the icy water near the pass. On Superior we carried a sail. On the Coppermine, heavy-duty plastic liners for each pack allowed half a foot of water to slosh around without damage to cargo in the heavy rapids. For going upstream in Barren Lands rapids, ten-foot poles had to be flown in with the party.

The other two requirements are *skill* and *stamina,* both of which are important in selecting a crew.

Among canoeing techniques, white-water skill, the ability both to read and to cope with rapids, can be a factor in wilderness survival—though on an easy trip a novice can be put in the bow to pick up skill as he goes. Under dangerous conditions in long rapids, the party acts as a *team,* much as does an alpine party on the rope. Each canoe follows strictly the course set by the first canoe to enter; thus, if Number One meets trouble, Number Two can correct the course, and the rest all benefit. In the descent of heavy rapids, the canoe should be slowed by back-paddling to no more than the speed of the current, which keeps out the worst of the waves. In going upstream, where the current is too strong for paddling and yet does not call for a portage, two techniques are used. The first is *poling,* as practised in punting. The poler stands, and even in a canoe well ballasted with cargo, considerable skill and balance are needed. The river bottom needs to be firm. The ten-foot pole, shod with an iron ferrule, limits the depth in which poling can be accomplished. Where the water is too deep, yet the shore is reasonably clear of overhanging snags or brush, the canoe is *lined* (or tracked), that is, towed on a long line. Sometimes the steersman stays aboard for this, though the canoe can be manipulated through its course by means of just the lining ropes. Both poling and lining are more easily done on the inside shore of a bend, where there is less current and depth; but this requires frequent crossing of the river. To avoid being swept back in paddling across, the canoe is angled at roughly thirty degrees to the current in a "cross-ferry"—which creates enough eddy to counteract some of the force of the current.

The last, though far from least, requirement is *stamina.* Stamina is related, inversely, to standard of living. Americans and Canadians for this reason—as was brought out in tests among the international forces in the Korean war—are among the softest of people. The physical condition required of the wilderness traveller is not the bull strength of the wrestler; what is needed is the respiro-cardio-vascular efficiency of the long-distance runner. Size is not necessarily an advantage—in fact, sometimes to the contrary. The criteria of physical fitness on long canoe trips are such things as the ability to be on the road for ten hours a day, or to portage an eighty-five pound canoe a mile without resting. Smoking does not help; alcohol in moderation appears to be no serious handicap.

The attitude of Canadians to wilderness is undeniably coloured by their closeness in time to the frontier and by their closeness to wilderness everywhere around. To the pioneer, the wilderness was unfriendly: its trees had to be felled to make way for fields and settlement, its wild animals killed for food or for security to crops and herds. The pioneer in a life of toil had no energy to travel the wilderness unnecessarily; and few of the inhabitants of a northern nation after a long hard winter sought the wilderness for holidays. In all these attitudes, early Canadians obeyed deep-down instincts of primitive ancestors.

Now, as the tempo of the population explosion and of industrialization works up, wilderness assumes suddenly a new value. A new awareness comes of wilderness as an area for escape, for regeneration. With the population of North America now estimated to be doubling every thirty-five years, with unrestricted tourist invasion from across the border, with modern mobility, and the four-day week looming, a spectre haunts Canadians when they think of their parks in the year 2000.

This is the context for talking of wilderness travel. The pragmatic wilderness seeker simply goes farther and farther north, where rugged climate, rocky terrain, vastness and inaccessibility will protect certain areas of Canada for some years to come. For those who are prepared to face the challenge and pay the price, such areas can be enjoyed—until the helicopters, hovercraft, skidoos and other screaming, roaring monsters on fat, soft wheels take over.

The challenge of wilderness travel in Canada is two-edged: the personal challenge to *explore,* and the public challenge to *preserve*—while yet we are able.

Beaver pond and lodge, Burleigh Game Preserve, Ontario. Bruce Litteljohn

Beaver-cut trees, Haliburton region, Ontario. Bruce Litteljohn

Ouimet Canyon, near Thunder Bay, northwestern Ontario. Bruce Litteljohn

Female bighorn sheep, Jasper National Park, Alberta. Dr. Frank Wood

Barren Ground caribou, near Aberdeen Lake, Northwest Territories. Dalton Muir

Pronghorn antelope, southern Saskatchewan. Dalton Muir

Plains bison, Wood Buffalo National Park, Alberta. Dalton Muir–National Parks

Tundra in autumn, Ennadai Lake, Northwest Territories. William I. Campbell

Valley of the Ten Peaks, Banff National Park, Alberta. Robert R. Taylor

Unnamed lake, Palliser Range, Banff National Park, Alberta. Dalton Muir—National Parks

Mount Assiniboine, Mount Assiniboine Provincial Park, British Columbia. Michael Naughton

Mount Assiniboine, Mount Assiniboine Provincial Park, British Columbia. Michael Naughton

Dinosaur Provincial Park, Alberta. Dalton Muir–National Parks

Dinosaur Provincial Park, Alberta. Dalton Muir–National Parks

Sunrise, Dinosaur Provincial Park, Alberta. Dalton Muir–National Parks

Sand dune country, near Carberry, Manitoba. Robert R. Taylor

Wild grass, Lonely Lake, Quetico Provincial Park, Ontario. Bruce Litteljohn

Tundra blooms, Baffin Island, Northwest Territories. Ken Dudley

Arctic poppy, Shultz Lake, Thelon River, Northwest Territories. J. W. L. Goering

Alpine meadow, Mount Revelstoke National Park, British Columbia. Dalton Muir–National Parks

Moss and evening sun, Kawartha Lakes region, Ontario. C. B. Cragg

GEORGE WOODCOCK

Terror and Regeneration: The Wilderness in Art and Literature

To Canadians the wilderness has always been present as a physical immediacy and a state of mind. It has shaped our outlook, and in shaping our outlook it has given a special shape to our literature and our visual arts, especially painting. Its influence, as many critics have observed, has been double-sided. Rupert Brooke, a poet used to more humanized landscapes, once stared at the vast ramparts of the Rockies and expressed the divided feelings that men have so often experienced when confronting the more spectacular features of the Canadian wilderness: *These unmemoried heights are inhuman, or rather irrelevant to humanity.... They acknowledge claims neither of the soul nor of the body of man. He is a stranger, neither Nature's enemy nor her child. She is there alone, scarcely a unity in the heaped confusion of these crags, almost without grandeur among the chaos of earth.*

Yet this horrid and solitary wilderness is but one aspect. There is beauty here... the real beauty that is too sudden for human eyes and brings pain with its comfort.

What Brooke saw as a stranger has been woven into the modern Canadian artistic and literary consciousness. Canadians may write of cities and the life of cities, they may turn deliberately away from the representation of nature in their paintings, yet somewhere in their visions and their forms the wilderness will always lurk, as it lurked in the consciousness of Roy Daniells when he wrote of Winnipeg,

...encompassed round
By the wind-haunted country and wide winter...

or of the hero of Hugh MacLennan's *Barometer Rising* as he stood, after returning to Halifax from exile, and thought of the distances that lay beyond... *this anomalous land, this sprawling waste of timber and rock and water where the only living sounds were the footfalls of animals or the fantastic laughter of a loon, this empty tract of primordial silences and winds and erosions and shifting colours.*

Our greatest critic, and one of the world's best, Northrop Frye, has remarked that "everything that is central in Canadian writing seems to be marked by the imminence of the natural world." Frye sees terror, but also a peculiar sense of distance, as characteristics that have been transmitted to Canadian poetry, and Canadian painting as well, through the sense of the imminence of the natural world, which means also, of course, the sense of the closeness of the wilderness. But if a consciousness of the forbidding and the perilous in the wilderness has always haunted Canadians, so also has its fascination, and in his frank raucousness Robert W. Service expressed what other writers have rendered with infinite variations of subtlety and gravity.

The strong life that never knows harness;
The wilds where the caribou call;
The freshness, the freedom, the farness
O God! How I'm stuck on it all!

The Canadian wilderness has been a shifting entity, retreating as settlement develops, waiting on the edge of cultivation, returning when the marginal lands are abandoned. Even now, it can start a few miles from the centre of a Canadian metropolis, as it does in Vancouver, and can continue, broken only by rare highways and a few scattered hamlets, indefinitely toward the Arctic Sea. This combined availability and threat of the wilderness undoubtedly explains why almost every Canadian writer at some time feels obliged to make acknowledgement of its existence. Even the town-bred heroes of that most urban of our novelists, Mordecai Richler, find at times that the idea of the wilderness lays a compelling hand upon them, as in *The Apprenticeship of Duddy Kravitz,* where Duddy can only feel himself a Somebody when he finally possesses a remote lake in the Laurentians, to gain which he has trampled on friend and enemy alike.

To the first men who came with the gift of writing, Canada was all wilderness, and from the start it dominated the records of exploration that are our first literature. It greeted the Norse explorers, and appeared in the Karlsefni Saga as Markland, "a land with great forests and many animals"; and as Vinland. "There are mountains there, and the land was beautiful to see. They spent their time exploring, and stayed through the winter, which was a hard one."

In such a way, during the thousand years since the Norsemen came, have many men written of the Canadian wilderness, talking of its forests and mountains and animals, of its beauty, of the hardness of its climate, and of other things, including its immense distances, its incomparable vistas. Jacques Cartier, the first explorer after the Norsemen to record his voyages, saw the terror of it when he named Labrador "the land that God gave Cain," but he also stood on Mount Royal, above the Indian town of Hochelaga, and looked up the St. Lawrence into the heart of the land. "And as far as the eye can see, one sees that river, large and wide, which comes from the south-west and flows near three fine conical mountains which we estimated to be some leagues away."

The St. Lawrence was then the great highway to the wilderness (and "the country's ornament" as Champlain described it when, seventy years after Cartier, he in turn wrote of his voyages); it was the entry to what the French called and have continued to call the *pays d'en haut,* the land upstream, meaning at first all that lay beyond Montreal, and later, as the wilderness became more distant and man's knowledge of it more extended, the forests of the Precambrian Shield and the plains of the great northwest.

From the beginning the wilderness attracted some and repelled others. To men who settled, it was the enemy, whose forests were to be cut down and whose weather as far as possible to be shut out. To others it became above all a place of liberation, and when settled men in New France wrote about the *coureurs de bois*, the men who went to trade furs among the Indians, they also called them *libertins*, as if the words were synonymous. The *coureurs de bois* were rarely literary or even literate men, and we have few accounts of their adventures or their attitudes. The most notable is the *Voyages* of Pierre-Esprit Radisson, the renegade French fur trader who, with his brother-in-law the Sieur des Groseilliers (Mr. Gooseberry to his London acquaintances) led the English to Hudson Bay in 1668.

Radisson's *Voyages* is a combination of truth and tall tales concocted to impress the courtiers and the City of London merchants who invested in the early Hudson's Bay Company, but much of it is clearly authentic, and Radisson's accounts of travel in the forests north of Lake Superior give a vivid sense of the free life of the *coureur de bois*, and are supplemented by a very lively account of his capture as a youth by the Mohawks and his life among them. This was the first of a special wilderness genre, the journal of captivity and escape, represented in the later narratives of Alexander Henry and John Tanner, captives of the Indians during the eighteenth century, and of John Jewitt, who underwent a similar experience among the Nootka Indians of Vancouver Island from 1803 to 1805. Jewitt's account is the only one that really rivals Radisson's in interest and vividness.

Professionally more inclined to writing than the *coureurs de bois* were the missionaries who began to penetrate the wilderness early in the history of New France. Especially important among their writings is the *Jesuit Relations*, the record of missionary activities sent to France largely to attract financial support for proselytization. Apart from such dramatic episodes as the destruction of Huronia by the Iroquois and the martyrdom of Brébeuf, the *Relations* included some of the earliest accounts of the hardships Europeans endured when they first travelled in the Canadian wilderness, such as Father La Jeune's narrative of a winter journey with Indians in the 1630's. *To paint to you the hardships of the way, I have neither brush nor pen that could do it; they must be experienced in order to be appreciated....We did nothing but go up and go down; frequently we had to bend half-way over to pass under partly fallen trees, and step over others lying upon the ground whose branches sometimes knocked us over, gently enough to be sure, but always coldly, for we fell upon the snow. If it happened to thaw, oh God what suffering! It seemed to me I was walking over a road of glass which broke under my feet at every step.*

Early wilderness literature tended to be of this utilitarian kind, designed to convey information and relate experience; it was not until the mid-nineteenth century that the attributes of the wilderness were used to any great extent as material for the poet or novelist. Yet there is a good case to argue that the best Canadian prose before Confederation—with the possible exception of Judge Haliburton's works—is to be found in the narratives of men who between 1690 and about 1820 served the fur companies as explorers, and in the process virtually created the map of the Canadian West.

The first was Henry Kelsey, "the boy Henry Kelsey," who in 1690 set off with Indian companions on a journey from Hudson Bay to the Plains that lasted two winters. Kelsey was the first Englishman to travel the prairies, to encounter grizzly bear and musk ox, to see the Indians hunting bison; they hunted on foot, for the horse had not yet found its way north through the Mississippi country from Mexico. Kelsey, who wrote part of his journal in doggerel, was the first rhymester of the wilderness, and probably the first man to write English verse on the Canadian mainland (though there had been poets at work in the Newfoundland settlements seventy years before). These lines about the animals he saw give a fair idea of his qualifications as a poet:

The one is a black a Buffalo great,
Another is an outgrown Bear which is good meat.
His skin to get I have used all the means I can,
He is man's food & he makes food of man.
His hide they would not me it preserve,
But said it was a God & they should starve.

Kelsey's naïve literary pretensions were not shared by his fellow explorers. But their prose often rose above the merely informational, and at least three of the books written when the fur traders ruled the wilderness are among the true classics of travel. Alexander Mackenzie's *Voyages* describes with classic but effective restraint his journey down the river that bears his name to the Arctic Sea, and his pioneer crossing of Canada by land to the Pacific in 1793. David Thompson had a more complex and sensitive mind than Mackenzie, and his *Narrative of his Explorations in the Western Americas 1784-1812* not only recounts vividly the great survey trips on which Thompson mapped much of the Rockies and explored the Columbia, but also shows a close and sympathetic interest in the human and animal inhabitants of the wilderness. One feels nearer to the person of the explorer—and to the physical reality of the wilderness—in reading Thompson than in reading Mackenzie. But one feels even nearer to Samuel Hearne, whose *Journey to the Northern Ocean* describes the hard travels which between 1769 and 1772 took this Hudson Bay ship's mate wandering with Indian bands over the Barren Lands to the Arctic Sea. It is not merely the description of a pioneer journey—a journey that helped to establish the geography of the northern wilderness. It is also a self-revealing narrative in which Hearne presents some of the first realistic and truly individual portraits of Indians in literature. Hearne lived too long among the northern Indians to accept the eighteenth-century myth of the "noble savage," but this did not prevent his observing them with a sympathy bred of shared hardships, even when their actions—as in the massacre of the Eskimoes at Coppermine River—filled him with a sense of powerless horror.

During the nineteenth century a rich source of exploration narratives was the series of Arctic search expeditions that followed Sir John Franklin's disappearance in 1845. The idea of wilderness is always associated with that of land, and most of the books that emerged from this great network of Arctic journeying fall outside our subject since their writers went by sea. One who did not was Dr. John Rae, the Hudson's Bay man travelling by sleigh and boat, who describes in his *Narrative* how he found the clues that established Franklin's fate. Rae's importance as a wilderness traveller lay in the way he adapted to exploration the arts of survival developed by the Eskimoes and northern Indians; he was the first white man to live off the land during winter in the Barrens north of the treeline.

As the map filled out, explorers were replaced by travellers, and travellers by tourists. *The Great Lone Land* and *The Wild North Land,* the florid narratives of the British officer William Francis Butler who wandered through the "old west" at the time of the Red River Rising, were typical of later nineteenth-century travellers who still experienced the harshness of wilderness living. *The North-west Passage by Land* of Viscount Milton and Dr. Cheadle brings the first Victorian tourists bursting west from Upper Canada. Hundreds of lesser travel books were to follow, particularly after the C.P.R. was completed, describing journeys by rail from settlement to settlement through a wilderness that was traversed rather than experienced.

But a genuine wilderness literature based on direct experience survived in the often naïve memoirs of fishermen and big game hunters, in the writings of field naturalists with literary inclinations like Edward Seton Thompson, Fred Bodsworth and Roderick Haig-Brown (who also wrote an interesting wilderness novel, *From the Highest Hill),* and in the literature concerning those men—eccentrics according to the norms of settled existence—who made the wilderness a habitation and a way of life.

One of the most curious among them was George Stansfeld Belaney, alias Grey Owl. Belaney was something of a charlatan, a native of the English county of Sussex who posed as an Indian and found it profitable. Yet the Grey Owl books—which in the 1930's rivalled those of Mazo de la Roche in representing Canadian literature to the outside world—did more than express grandiose platitudes about the wilderness. ("And as the last dying echo fades to nothing, the silence settles layer by layer....") Belaney was capable of accuracy as well as empathy in describing the animals that peopled the wilderness to which, in his own way, he remained devoted.

More recently the literature of direct wilderness experience has been enriched by Farley Mowat's controversial books defending Northern losers—inland Eskimoes, wolves, and others—and by one of the most remarkable books on life beyond the settlements ever written in Canada, George Whalley's *The Legend of John Hornby.* John Hornby was a man not especially fitted for life in the North, indifferent in physique and inefficient in some of the vital techniques of wilderness living, but he was compulsively attracted to the landscapes and the privations of the Barren Lands, and he put himself to one test of survival after another until, after twenty years of it, he died of starvation in a cabin on the Thelon River. Using documents and the recollections of men who had known Hornby, Whalley created a narrative as stark as its setting, and as stark as the tales of courage in extreme situations that Camus wrote.

The literature of direct experience of the wilderness has continued in an unbroken tradition since Cartier. It is writing as the product of action. Writing as action for its own sake began very precariously in the settlements of the Maritimes and along the St. Lawrence, and the earliest Canadian men of letters tended to reflect the attitudes of the settlers to whom the wilderness was a world to be feared, repelled, never to be accepted. One of the most durable books about the Upper Canadian wilderness has been Susanna Moodie's *Roughing It in the Bush,* and Susanna's tone when she wrote of pioneering in the forest was one of bitter eloquence. In Nova Scotia, Joshua Marsden wrote in 1827: *There is . . . a solitary loneliness in the woods of North America to which no language can do adequate justice. It seems a shutting out of the whole moral creation.*

Standish O'Grady, a little later, was even harsher in his reaction, and matched Voltaire's "few *arpents* of snow" with equally disdainful lines:

> *Here forests crowd, unprofitable lumber,*
> *O'er fruitless lands indefinite as number.*

And apart from the forest, there was the weather, of which, in that first of all Canadian novels, *The History of Emily Montague,* Frances Brooke wrote in 1767 that "the rigour of the climate suspends the very powers of the understanding; what then must become of those of the imagination?"

Among early Canadians the eighteenth-century distaste for wild nature was prolonged by the hardships of pioneering, and only occasionally did a writer break into an expression of romantic thrill, like Anna Jamieson, sailing beside the shores of Georgian Bay—then totally untamed—and hearing the news of Queen Victoria's accession from a passing boat. The sun rises at this moment opportunely over the lake, and Anna responds. *The idea that even here, in this new world of woods and shores, amid these remote wilds, to her so utterly unknown, her power reaches and her sovereignty is acknowledged, filled me with compassionate awe. . . . And what a fair heritage is this that has fallen to her! A land young like herself—a land of hopes—and fair, most fair! Does she know—does she care anything about it?—while hearts are beating warm for her and voices bless her and hands are stretched out towards her even from these wild lake shores.*

The real awakening of writers to the wilderness as part of an imaginative heritage coincided with the upsurge of national feeling that preceded Confederation. For the first time Canadians other than fur traders and voyageurs began to look beyond their lakeshores, and their curiosity was especially embodied in the Canada First movement. One of the most enthusiastic Canada Firsters was the poet Charles Mair, who went west at the time of the Red River Rising and reacted with deep emotion to his first view of the prairie. *There the awful solitude opens upon the sight and swells into an ocean, and the eye wanders over the "silent space" of the West. The man must be corrupt as death who, unaccustomed, can look unmoved upon this august material presence, this calm unutterable vastness.*

> *. . . We left*
> *The silent forest, and, day after day,*
> *Great prairies swept beyond our aching sight*
> *Into the measureless West; uncharted realms,*
> *Voiceless and calm, save when tempestuous wind*
> *Rolled the rank herbage into billows vast,*

And rushing tides which never found a shore....
The deep-grooved bison-paths like furrows lay,
Turned by the cloven hoofs of thundering herds
Primeval, and still travelled as of yore.
And gloomy valleys opened at our feet—
Shagged with dusk cypresses and hoary pine....

Mair's fascination with the wilderness was taken up by better poets, particularly by Isabella Valancy Crawford and Duncan Campbell Scott. Isabella Valancy Crawford never experienced anything beyond an Ontario that in her day was already tamed and settled, but the tales of the wilderness struck her imagination, and she made of them a secret world of fantasy in poems like "Old Spookses' Pass" and "Said the Canoe," in which the Indian hunters

Into the hollow hearts of brakes—
Yet warm from sides of does and stags
Passed to the crisp, dark river-flags—
Sinuous, red as copper-snakes,
Sharp-headed serpents, made of light,
Glided and hid themselves in night.

Duncan Campbell Scott, on the other hand, was one of the few poets of his time who knew the wilderness from direct experience. He served for more than fifty years in the Department of Indian Affairs, and his work took him into the wild settings that not long before had been visited only by fur traders, so that he saw the life of the Indians as a stark conflict between man and nature, but also as a way of existence doomed by history. Some of his most moving poems, like "The Forsaken" (of a women doomed by the tribe because she had become old and useless) were inspired by this social perception. Others sprang out of a pure apprehension of the wilderness as a place of beauty, and in poems like "En Route" he writes of it with a sharp and almost imagist clarity.

The train has stopped for no apparent reason
In the wilds;
A frozen lake is level and fretted over
With rippled wind lines;
The sun is burning in the South; the season
Is winter trembling at a touch of spring.
A little hill with birches and a ring
Of cedars—all so still, so pure with snow—
It seems a tiny landscape in the moon.
Long wisps of shadow from the naked birches
Lie on the white in lines of cobweb-grey;
From the cedar roots the snow has shrunk away.
One almost hears it tinkle as it thaws,
Traces there are of wild things in the snow—
Partridge at play, tracks of the foxes' paws
That broke a path to sun them in the trees.
They're going fast where all impressions go
On a frail substance—images like these,
Vagaries the unconscious mind receives
From nowhere and lets go to nothingness
With the lost flush of last year's autumn leaves.

Scott was a great deal more than a wilderness poet. He was a versatile writer moved by the wilderness as he was by many other aspects of existence. Indeed, one of the striking aspects of Canadian literature since Confederation has been that the best imaginative writing about the wilderness has occurred in occasional poems and in fictional episodes by writers whose scope extended far beyond the wilderness itself.

After the Klondike Gold Rush at the end of the nineteenth century there was a great fashion for novels about logging, mining, trapping, the Mounties and other aspects of wilderness life, but very few of them are now remembered and even fewer are read. Occasional books of this type like Martin Allerdale Grainger's *Woodsmen of the West* retain enough interest to be reprinted, and academics still discuss writers like Frederick Niven, though few other people read them. But in general the novels about the wilderness that were nothing more than inventive records of action have weathered far worse than explorers' narratives and the better travel books, for the good reason that action always comes off best when it is described straightforwardly. The novel of action fails because it puts a screen of contrivance between us and what actually happened.

The imaginative writers who turned the wilderness to a real literary purpose were those who applied values different from or perhaps extra to those of the explorers. In the exploration narratives the wilderness is presented as a physical experience, often with moral overtones suggesting that the life of forests and barrens is freer than life in cities and hence superior. Sometimes—I think David Thompson is an example—the explorer begins to apply aesthetic criteria to discuss the wilderness in terms of its visual appeal. The imaginative writer accepts the physical and moral aspects of the wilderness experience, extends the aesthetic aspect—as Scott does in the poem I have quoted—and often adds a philosophic dimension, relating what he sees to the workings of a universe he might otherwise find incomprehensible and to a human condition that also gains in meaning when it is related to the images of the natural world.

This turning toward the wilderness is the understandable termination of a stage of development in which men have ceased to be pioneers, regarding the wilderness as a natural enemy, and have come to feel that its loss may have cut them off from a necessary aspect of existence. Thus there are many writers in whose work the wilderness plays a relatively small part in terms of pages, but a vital part in terms of illumination. Works based on a confrontation with the natural world which have a special importance in defining their writers' outlooks are novels like Gabrielle Roy's *La Montagne Secrète* and Yves Thériault's *Ashini,* and poems like Earle Birney's "David," Douglas Le Pan's "Canoe-Trip," A. J. M. Smith's "The Lonely Land," and A. W. Purdy's *North of Summer.* Nor should one forget that best of all Frederick Philip Grove's books, *Over Prairie Trails,* in which he shows how the wilderness returns in winter to dominate the great plains which its enemies, the farmers, rule in summer.

Even more interesting are the instances of major Canadian novels in which the wilderness is used at some point to stress the central meaning of the work. In Hugh MacLennan's *The Watch that Ends the Night,* Jerome Martell's childhood in the New Brunswick forest comes as a great flashback to illuminate the whole of his life's actions.

And in Morley Callaghan's *They Shall Inherit the Earth*, a hunting expedition ends in a scene that symbolizes the wilderness in the heart of the hero who has let his father bear public blame for a death that was his responsibility. *They crossed the deer trails and were out on the hard crust, and when they had gone a little way they saw that the mound was really the carcass of a deer. There were many other carcasses, and blood marks, with the snow churned up, and the carcasses stuck there in the hard crust; the sharp hoofs of the deer, piercing through the crust, had impaled them in the snow. A deer stuck stiff in the snow is very dead; there is nothing quite so dead. The carcasses were slashed at the throat, or slashed at the nose, and the flesh of the tenderloin had been torn from every one of the carcasses, just the nice juicy tenderloin torn away, and the rest of the carcass left there to bleed and freeze in the snow.*

This passage of Callaghan seems to epitomize the terror that Northrop Frye had seen as one aspect of the Canadian writer's reaction to his land. But it is a terror that looks inward as well as outward. For Callaghan's wolves roam the human mind as well as the inhuman waste.

The relationship between Canadian painting and the wilderness has followed a course very similar to that between writing and the wilderness, and often the writers and painters have been the same persons. A. Y. Jackson (in *A Painter's Country*) and Emily Carr (in *Klee Wyck*) have both written books that were unique contributions to the literature of the wilderness, and one of the earliest books of real interest written about the "old West" by someone other than a fur trader was Paul Kane's *Wanderings of an Artist*. Kane, in 1846, was the first professional painter to set out for the West in search of material; his only predecessor in the region, Peter Rindisbacher, had gone there as a Swiss immigrant to join the Selkirk Colony on the Red River in 1821, and had left some interesting primitive paintings of Indians and fur traders. Before Kane the professional painters of Eastern Canada had shared the settlers' prejudices about the wilderness, and had followed the prevailing taste by painting humanized landscapes; when, like Joseph Légaré, they did compose canvases showing Indians lurking in forests, these were contrived in the studio with the help of romantic imaginations. The artists who at this early time did show some interest in the natural landscape were British officers who came after the conquest, with some training in topographical draughtsmanship which they sometimes used to portray the wilder countrysides. Thomas Davies, who worked about 1760, has recently been recognized as a minor master, showing in his paintings of Canadian woods, rivers and Indian encampments a naïve, illuminist vision which some critics have likened to that of the Douanier Rousseau. Another fine but less idiosyncratic topographical artist was Sir George Back, who made some very evocative drawings of the northern forests and the Barren Lands when he accompanied Franklin's 1825 expedition to the Arctic Sea.

Kane's attitude, like that of the topographers, was primarily documentary; he set out to record the Indians in their wild state, and he succeeded, but the styles he used were conventionally heroic—stiff-legged horses and noble warriors—as were those of his disciple Frederick Verner who reached the plains in the 1870's to paint the last of the buffalo, and to set on canvas the treaties by which the Indians of the Prairies abdicated their freedom of the wilderness. A more aesthetic approach was adopted by one of the most curious western painters, William G. R. Hind. Hind learned his art among the English Pre-Raphaelites, and when he decided to travel with the Overlanders across Canada to the Cariboo goldfields he painted the Rockies on the way with the meticulous detail characteristic of his school, and made drawings of Cariboo taverns filled with bearded miners who looked as though they had strayed out of a medieval epic by William Morris.

By the 1870's, painters were appearing who had realized that the atmospheric conditions and the colours of the Canadian wilderness required special treatments, and as early as the 1870's Allan Edson, in wilderness settings of forests and waterfalls, experimented with the effects of light in a way that anticipated the work of the Impressionists in Europe. The completion of the Canadian Pacific Railway in 1886 set a whole company of artists foot-loose among the Rockies and beyond, encouraged by that great connoisseur, Sir William Van Horne, and some of them, like Mower Martin, produced memorable sketches of the mountains and anticipated Emily Carr by painting the dramatic villages of the Coast Indians, with their carved poles and painted house fronts.

But undoubtedly the most important movement into the wilderness in the history of Canadian painting was that of the Group of Seven in the years before and after the First World War. The Group of Seven did not emerge from an artistic vacuum. Other artists before them, like Charles W. Jefferys, who painted the remoter and more untamed parts of the Prairies at the turn of the century, had already sketched out the attitudes which the Group of Seven developed. "It is inevitable," said Jefferys, "that a country with such marked physical characteristics as Canada possesses should impress itself forcefully upon our artists." And it is unlikely that the Group of Seven would have developed as it did without the influence of Tom Thomson, who combined artistic genius with the talents of a fine woodsman, who first discovered the painting possibilities of the wilder parts of Ontario, and who began to develop the style that would render this landscape into paintings whose striking colours and tense outlines gave expression to the uniqueness of the Canadian wilderness.

Thomson died too early to fulfil his splendid promise, lost like Blair Fraser in the waters of the wilderness he loved. His friends and his disciples, in search for a source of art in the untamed natural setting, continued his task. A. Y. Jackson, Lawren Harris, Arthur Lismer, J. E. H. MacDonald, Frederick Varley, Franklin Carmichael—never before had such a group of vigorous painters been impelled with such a missionary urge to give original expression to the magnificent surface of the Canadian land. From their original base in Georgian Bay they spread to the northern shores of Lake Superior, and—some of them at least—to the Rockies and the Yukon, the Pacific and the Arctic. As they developed it was clear that they were as different as good painters inevitably must be, yet there was enough similarity among their work to make it obvious that a MacDonald painting of Georgian Bay belonged to the same school as a Jackson painting of the same region, and together they established a collective image of the Canadian wilderness so strong that they almost proved Oscar Wilde's old paradox about nature imitating art; it is hard, even now, to look at an autumn scene in Algoma or north of Sault Ste. Marie and not to see it as a Group of Seven landscape.

The Seven established among Canadian painters a preoccupation with landscape which even the recent triumph of international abstractionist and pop-and-op styles has not entirely overwhelmed. The immediate successors of the Group remained close interpreters of the natural environment, David Milne establishing his own private and miniature wilderness among the Ontario hills and Emily Carr creating her green conflagrations out of the gloomy forests of British Columbia. And many painters who are now prominent in Canada passed through stages of painting in the wilderness—as Jack Shadbolt and Gordon Smith and Bruno Bobak and Jacques de Tonnancour and many others have all done in their time—and in the work they do today the forms learnt from its landscapes are still dominant even in disguise. As to what they have found in the wilderness, it has probably been said best by the poet A. J. M. Smith.

This is a beauty
of dissonance
this resonance
of stony strand,
this smoky cry
curled over a black pine
like a broken
and wind-battered branch
when the wind
bends the tops of the pines
and curdles the sky
from the north.

This is the beauty
of strength
broken by strength
And still strong.

Shield rock and white pine, evening, Doe Island, Stoney Lake, Ontario. Bruce Litteljohn

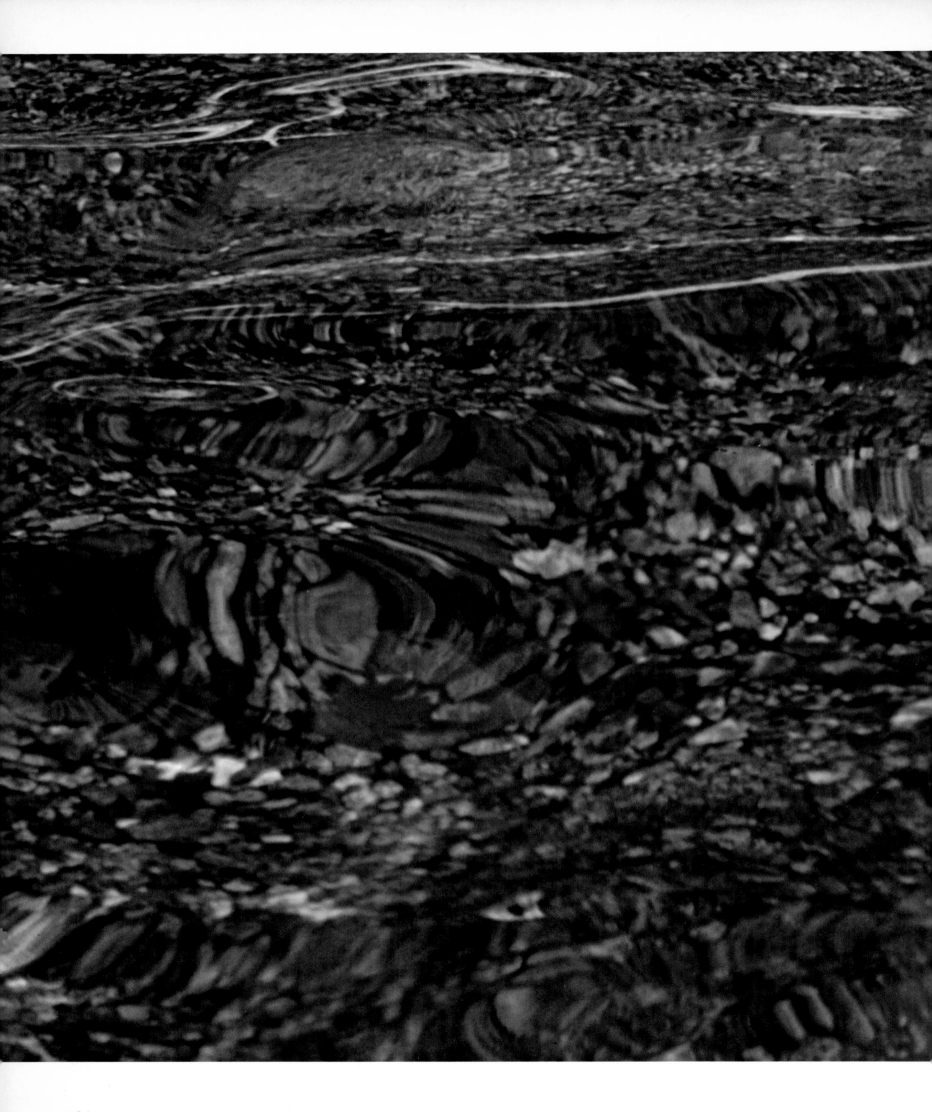

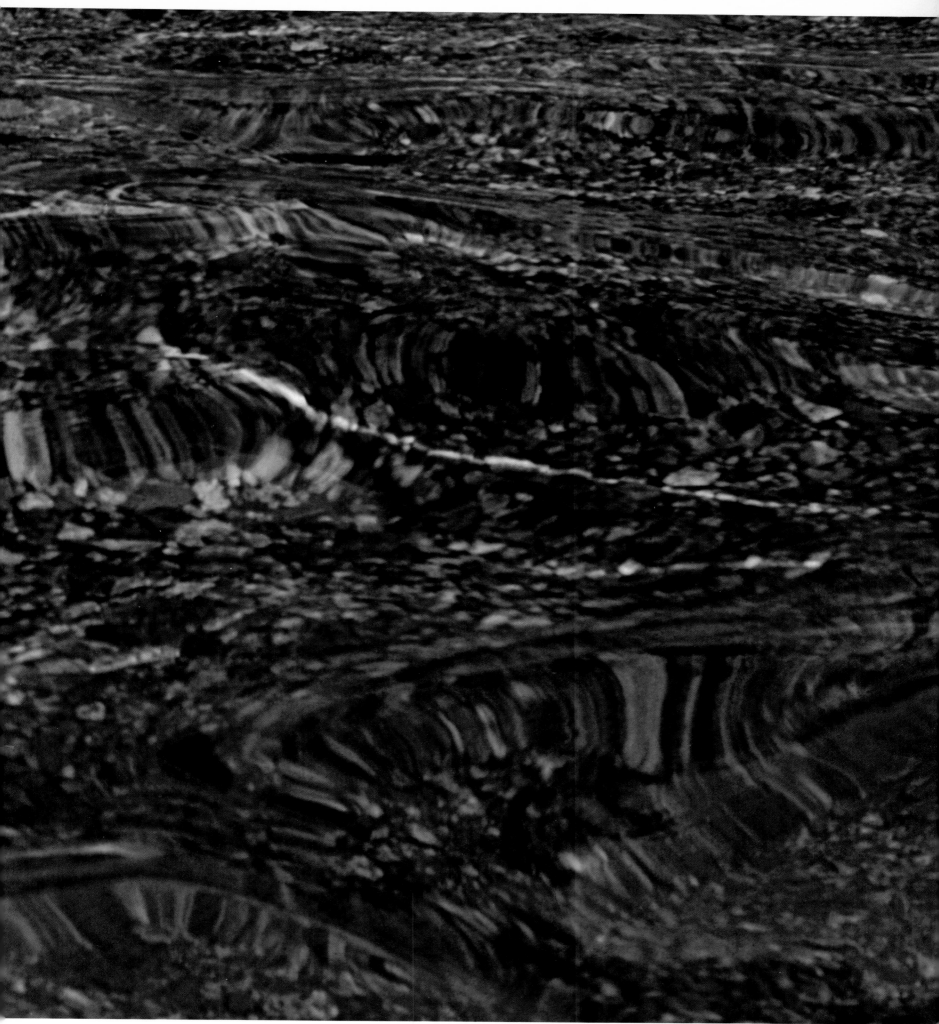

O.S.A. Lake, Killarney Provincial Park, Ontario. John G. Foster

Lichen-covered tamarack, near Kenora, Ontario. Robert R. Taylor

Mushrooms, Sturgeon Lake, Quetico Provincial Park, Ontario. Bruce Litteljohn

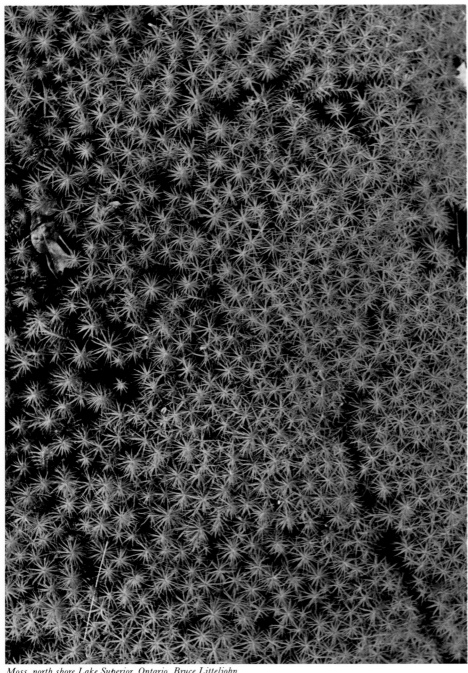

Moss, north shore Lake Superior, Ontario. Bruce Litteljohn

Spider web, Beaverhouse Lake, Quetico Provincial Park, Ontario. Bruce Litteljohn

Spider and web, Windigoostigwan Lake, Rainy River District, Ontario. Bruce Litteljohn

Hoarfrost on highbush cranberry, Ontario. William D. Addison

Western rain forest, north of Vancouver, British Columbia. Robert R. Taylor

Morning mist in boreal forest, Caliper Lake, northwestern Ontario. Robert R. Taylor

Ruffed grouse eating willow catkins, near Kenora, Ontario. Robert R. Taylor

Rain forest, northwest of Nanaimo, Vancouver Island, British Columbia. Robert R. Taylor

Close-up of liverworts, Quetico Provincial Park, Ontario. Jack Hasse

Near Baddeck, Cape Breton Island, Nova Scotia. Dalton Muir

Common loon, near Perth, Ontario. Dalton Muir

Hottah Lake, Northwest Territories. Paul Baich–National Film Board

Ptarmigan cock in winter plumage at edge of tundra lake, Northwest Territories. Fred Bruemmer

Storm clouds over Doré Lake, Rainy River District, northwestern Ontario. Bruce Litteljohn

114

JOHN A. LIVINGSTON

Man and His World: A Dissent

Wilderness conservation has always been a difficult concept for us to grasp, because we resist "identifying" with nature. We have always had reluctance to see a tract of land which is empty of men as anything but a void. The "waste howling wilderness" of Deuteronomy is typical. The Oxford Dictionary defines wilderness as wild or uncultivated land which is occupied "only" by wild animals. Places not used by us are "wastes." Areas not occupied by us are "desolate." Could the desolation be in the soul of man?

If a place that is uninhabited by man is the true wilderness, what does it become when man appears? It is possible that man and wilderness are mutually exclusive. There was a time—and it is still true in some remote parts of the world—when hunting-and-gathering man was a functioning member of the natural community. When he took up permanent settlements, a part of wild nature ceased to exist. The pure definition of wilderness, then, is ideally the absence of man, or his presence only in limited numbers, as an integrated part of the fauna. To what extent this applies to our increasing recreational use of wilderness is an open question.

Our definitions of wilderness have connotations over and above the mere presence or absence of man. In such words as "wasteland," "desolation" and "wilderness," there are implied threats to our physical safety. It is trite to say that we fear what we do not know and cannot see, but the fears are no less real for that. Our anxiety has long traditions, both biological and cultural.

It did not begin at any precise instant in time, but it was millions of years ago, probably on the plains of Africa. Then as now, the wide savannah supported the most remarkable array of large animals the world has ever seen—plant-eaters and meat-eaters, living together harmoniously; elephants, gazelles, rhinoceroses, giant giraffes, big cats, coursing dogs. Among them were groups of furtive, tentative little creatures nervously moving about, always on the alert. Poorly equipped for defence (they had not yet developed weapons), these small primates depended almost exclusively on their eyesight for moment-to-moment security. They lived something like modern baboons, except that they habitually used an erect stance on two legs to peer over the grasses.

A forest with its near-zero visibility and an abundance of hiding places for the ancestral leopard was clearly no place for a small primate, once it had become terrestrial. Having come down from the trees in the first place, our ancestors felt it imperative to get as far away from them as possible. We still fear dark or confined places, where our eyes cannot help us; we fear places which lack the company of others of our kind. The house cat and the tiger are solitary, and go their own way; the baboon is gregarious, and a man alone in the wilderness is a lost soul. Our genetic memory is long.

As modern man evolved, from the African grassland to the mountains and valleys of Europe and Asia, the old apprehensions were passed down through the generations. Neolithic man staring into the blackness beyond his fire saw in the flickering, shifting shadows all the indefinable foreboding to which his descendants later gave expression in the Black Forest. The spine-tingling tales of the brothers Grimm nearly always had to do with deep, impenetrable forests. (The two words seem to be inseparable. In Uganda there is an area called the Impenetrable Forest, even though a road cuts through it now.)

The forests were not only impenetrable; they were magic, supernatural. They were evil. Could anything be more chilling than Blake's tiger "in the forests of the night"? Or Longfellow's "Dark behind it rose the forest,/Rose the black and gloomy pine-trees"?

When white men came to North America they brought with them their European culture, including their fears. They also brought the Judaeo-Christian code, which can be interpreted as to assure us that the earth and everything upon it were created for the sole and exclusive use, benefit and rule of man. (There are still those who believe it.) When they arrived, they already had a predisposition about the wilderness, and they found a lot of wilderness. It was hostile and malevolent, but after all it was for their domination. That was the only possible reason for its existence. They feared the wilderness, but their duty was to fight it, subdue it and exploit it as quickly and thoroughly as they could.

That these ancient attitudes toward our living environment still persist among the unquestioning boosters, the promoters, the Babbitts, the developers, and so many politicians and even intellectuals is a regrettable relic of the past. Such attitudes are at the core of the impending world environmental crisis. Our Old Testament philosophy, with its roots in pre-history, dies hard. The crucial question is whether it will die in time for us to preserve some measure of quality in human existence. Wilderness is part of that quality.

There is an interesting sidelight to the nature tradition in Canada. Ask someone to identify the Canadian wilderness, and almost without exception he will name the northern forest. Rarely will he think of the Arctic. Although the Arctic and subarctic represent the greater part of the remaining true Canadian wilderness, we continue to think in terms of vast stands of trees—uninhabited, for the most part, by people. The north is epitomized by the raven, and the wolf. And by stillness.

Wilderness exists in the north, plenty of it. But it is remarkable how pocked it is already by the first manifestations of civilization. A map of oil-well exploration, for example, is startling. A map of mining claims, or of forestry operations and leases, is enlightening. The initial

116

penetration has been made in the northern wilderness, and there is an uncomfortable feeling of the beginning of the end. At the edge of any clearing, the deterioration of nature is depressingly evident. As the Scottish ecologist Frank Fraser Darling has put it, a forest must have a good skirt. "If you can begin to see a forest's knees, something is wrong; it is much better that it should have a skirt well down to the ground. The shanks of a lodgepole should not be seen from outside."

We can see the shanks of the forest too easily. Tiny peepholes are appearing throughout the north. They have a way of fraying, and widening, with time. This is a critical problem, because in order for them to exist in a healthy state wilderness areas must be much more extensive than we used to realize.

Darling describes it this way: "Wilderness is scarcely ever large enough now to be left utterly and absolutely alone. Wilderness has edges, and it is on the edges that you get wear from the outside. There is impingement all the time." Vast as the Canadian wilderness is, it is faced with impingement from the outside, and from the inside. Each mine, each mill, each oil rig is the nucleus of wear from within. As each nucleus expands inexorably, and is joined to the next by air routes, rails and roads, the "wilderness" comes to resemble nothing so much as a massive hull riddled by shipworm. It is difficult to sustain any longer the old concept of Canada's "limitless" wilderness. The limitless wilderness was a thing of the past with the first bush plane.

If we are concerned about the preservation of wilderness, or at least of substantial parts of it, sooner or later we must ask ourselves why. In view of what we have always believed about man's appointed role on earth, why preserve wilderness? Who in the world needs it?

Three thousand million years ago, in some calm and broth-like sea, the living wilderness was sparked. A single-celled being became the progenitor of the spruce tree and the arethusa orchid, the porcupine and the whisky jack, the wolf, and you. Wilderness and its inhabitants are the end product at this particular moment of all these millennia of the beauty and grandeur of the evolutionary process. A species of tree or bird or mammal, of course, is simply an arbitrary and convenient expression of a point in time. Evolution is dynamic, and the species we recognize today may not be recognizable tomorrow. For its continuance, evolution needs all the living elements that make up wilderness.

We may have admiration—even awe—of the majestic forces which brought us to this moment, of the clean order which runs through the bewildering complexity of biological events. But we have great difficulty seeing ourselves in that perspective. We are relatively unmoved by the history of life, which is really little more than a long list of extinctions. We know that this is proper, and that evolution depends upon extinctions for its advancement. We forget, however, that natural extinctions take tens of thousands of years, and we ignore the fact that because of human activities a species of bird or mammal has become extinct for every year of this century, an unnatural acceleration in the rate. And of course we are quite incapable of envisaging or even entertaining the thought of the extinction of man.

Our blindness to our own biological context compels us to view extinction in a perspective which we can comprehend, such as that (possibly) of the whooping crane, or perhaps the Sumatran rhinoceros. We can feel sorry about these. The day of the whooping crane, we can say, seems to be past, and that is too bad, but that is the way it is. We seem to be utterly oblivious to the enormity of the fact that with the extinction of any form of life we see the brutally abrupt end of a process that began billions of years ago (in the same instant that we ourselves began), the termination of a unique series of accidental genetic events which can never take place again. That is the horror of *preventable* extinctions. Where do we achieve the depth of perception necessary to understand what it is we do when we invade the wilderness—*all* of the wilderness?

The wilderness is finite. David Brower of the Sierra Club has expressed it this way: "There is no substitute for wilderness. What we now have is all that we ever shall have." That is the practical fact we must admit, and the obligation we must recognize. What we see fit to save now will be all that is left of the work of the forces that some of us call God. All, that is, save man, whose appropriateness as the exemplary product of evolution (or Creation) remains to be confirmed. Nature existed long before there was man, and nature needs at least a vestigial reservoir of wilderness from which once again to populate the planet in wonderful diversity—in the due passage of time.

At present there are many forms of wildlife whose existence depends entirely on large tracts of inviolate wilderness. Some, like the wolf, by their nature are incompatible with man, either because man fears them, or because man vigorously dominates them. There is no substitute for Arctic wilderness for the existence of walrus and polar bear. There is no substitute for forest wilderness for the existence of marten, fisher, wolverine, cougar, Canada lynx and woodland caribou.

Some animals need great spaces, remoteness from man and his works. These are not the likes of raccoons, grey squirrels, rats and house sparrows—even white-tailed deer—which can live with and even benefit from human activities. Wilderness species are a breed apart; their aloofness is special. The very fact of their vulnerability to human encroachment somehow ennobles them.

Man needs wilderness too, even though it may seem a contradiction. The point at which recreational use of wilderness defeats its own purpose is difficult to isolate. It varies with the individual. To some purists, the landing of one pontoon aircraft on a remote northern lake is the end of that particular wilderness. Canoeists and other primitive-trippers are not delighted to encounter others intent on the same private experience. How many visitors constitute the end of wilderness?

The feeling of wilderness is obviously subjective and very personal. At the other end of the scale from the purist is the man who is content to limit his experience to the crowded Lake of Two Rivers campsite in Algonquin Park on a summer weekend. This may be as close to the wilderness as he ever wants to be. Indeed he may believe that he has been there. If he takes home the memory of a loon's wail, who is to say that he has not touched the wilderness?

But aesthetics to the side, we need wilderness for practical reasons. It is the last refuge of the natural and unencumbered interactions of living things. With the diminution of wilderness we lose an irreplaceable laboratory—the very stuff of knowledge. There is an illustration of this which has often been used: let it be remembered that man does not synthesize antibiotics. They are produced by living microorganisms. Who knows what remains to be discovered in the complexity of nature—or what has already been lost? Richard Pough has repeatedly made the point that when an ecosystem of any size is lost, the raw material of biology goes with it. Daniel B. Beard remarks, "The scientist must work in the living community, where the interplay of nature is unfettered. Later on, it can be carried from the field to the laboratory for experimentation, perfection, and adaptation for use."

We are only beginning to realize the full impact on our environment of residual chemical poisons such as DDT. That it has contaminated the entire biosphere is known; its effects on wilderness species such as the bald eagle and the peregrine falcon are known, and are in the process of being understood. It may be callous and human-centred to say this, but without animal species to study, whether in the wild or in captivity, we might never apprehend the total horror of environmental pollution—until too late. Ecology is a young science, but already it indicates the future of mankind. The study of human ecology depends utterly on natural situations in which to examine the multiplicity of forces and factors which direct our lives. We destroy nature and wilderness at our own very grave peril.

Despite our human self-interest, however, there is an ethic about wilderness. Most people will never see a cougar or a golden eagle, and many do not especially care whether they do, but a surprising number of them take an irrational comfort in knowing that they are still with us, somewhere. The same applies to wilderness as a whole. If indeed there is a Canadian "identity," it is (at least in most other countries) closely identified with wilderness. We may not care for this image—the chambers of commerce do not—but it is one of the things that sets this country apart from so many others. It is the wilderness aura—the cleanness, the openness, the vitality of the north.

I appreciate the teen-age girl who told me that she values the Canadian wilderness, even though she has no interest in going there. She would do whatever she could to help preserve it, however, for its own sake, as a kind of ideal. There is more practical value in this point of view than might seem. Man is an animal, true enough, with an undeniable biological heritage. But he is also the animal who can recognize that not every expression of the human spirit need be a human artifact. Wilderness preservation is every bit as much a tribute to human nature as any poem; it takes the same measure of sensibility to cherish either.

We have seen that evolution needs wilderness, and that both wildlife and mankind need wilderness. Industry also needs it. The first impact of industry comes with exploration. With bush planes, prospectors' camps, tracked vehicles and snowmobiles, the imprint of invasion is on the land long before any significant "development" takes place, and the wilderness is never quite the same again. Runaway campfires can destroy caribou lichens over wide areas for as much as seventy-five years. Vehicle tracks on the delicate muskeg may remain indefinitely. The scars are there long before the appearance of buildings and the other more permanent trappings of industry.

Air and water pollution follow—in the wilderness, largely unchecked. Power dams (so often politically tainted) on primeval rivers destroy immense areas of woodland, and their inhabitants. Our record of land-use in the southern parts of the country, such as the lamented Niagara Peninsula and the Fraser River, leads one to despair of anything but the most unplanned and piecemeal approach to priorities in the exploitation of the "limitless" north. We seem to make the same mistakes, over and over again.

Tourist invasion by aircraft, outboard motor and snowmobile leaves traces just as unsightly, just as permanent. Our only hope of preventing the defacement of much of the north will be a widespread structure of *wilderness* parks or other preserves, which will be closed to access by any mechanical means. Transportation will be limited to canoe, horse or one's own legs. It is not only the oil slicks and motor fumes which offend the wilderness traveller; *noise* pollution is becoming one of the serious psychic nuisances of our time.

The Industrial Revolution encouraged us to believe unhesitatingly and even fervently in the equation between production and progress. We have not changed. The conventional wisdom permeating government, commerce and industry is still exemplified in the Gross National Product. Production and consumption, at a spiralling rate of increase, keep the economy moving. To interrupt or stall the cycle would be disastrous. One seriously wonders about a society in which standard of living (which means the ostentatious display of the appurtenances of affluence) is placed before *quality* of living—including the very air we breathe. Wilderness is only one of the qualities of living, but it is a vital one. If the conventional wisdom should be allowed to continue obscuring the ecological wisdom, it could well be suicidal.

It is in human nature to be acquisitive, whether for cash and goods or for a fishing trophy, or even for a wilderness experience. No doubt the growing pressures of our urban environment will cause greater and greater numbers of us to yearn for the physical and spiritual resuscitation which can only be achieved in fresh air, and silence. That will pose a significant problem. We are already loving our recreational parks to bits; we must not allow ourselves to do it to the remaining wilderness.

Clearly we cannot police ourselves voluntarily; some sort of regulatory control of access to wild areas is inevitable. Regulation compounded on regulation is anathema to all of us, but there seems no reasonable alternative. It will not be easy. The jurisdictional tangles surrounding public lands are so complex that one despairs of a clean-cut solution. Any one of us may be a citizen of a number of governments, and one parcel of land may be influenced by a seemingly infinite number of public agencies. In the final analysis, who will be responsible for what? From experience, one could say that the higher the level of government, the healthier the prospect for conservation.

It is as suspect to question the freedom of private enterprise as it is to be against motherhood (although in view of the world population crisis the latter point of view is becoming increasingly respectable). The freedom of enterprise does not carry with it the licence to exploit wherever, whenever, however business considers it desirable. There will be stricter regulations in this field. Land-use planning must of necessity state ecologically-biased priorities which will indicate what in fact is the best use of a given block of land. Surprisingly, often the best

use is not "development." Control of the industrialization of the Canadian north will require the emergence of a singularly brave new breed of politicians.

This may not be as unrealistic as it sounds. Politicians are not the craven lackeys of big business; they are the representatives of the people. In order to be elected, any politician consciously reflects what he believes to be the wishes of a majority of his constituents. Much more often than not, he is a mirror of the public conscience. That the electorate has not heretofore expressed itself forcibly in conservation matters is regrettable. The fault is not in our stars, but in ourselves.

We might not be in quite so critical a situation with respect to wild lands were it not for the B.N.A. Act, under the terms of which these matters are largely under the control of the provinces. In order for a national park to be established, for example, the province must deed land to the federal government with no strings attached. Some provinces have done better than others in this regard. Ontario, for example, has seen fit to permit the existence of a grand total of twelve square miles of national parks in that immense province. The excuse is given that this is compensated for by the provincial parks, of which there is a good number. When one considers, however, the commercial logging operations in Ontario parks, there is a certain justifiable fear about wild lands in provincial ownership. This fear is amplified by reference to the record of the province of British Columbia.

One of the frustrating aspects of the wilderness preservation movement as a whole is the difficulty of identifying a sufficient number of people who care enough to take co-ordinated political or other action. The greatest population centres in the country are a long way (both physically and temporally) from the wilderness, and there is an abundance of distractions. It is difficult for people to take you seriously, in the luxury of an elegant Montreal restaurant, when you express concern about the future of the grizzly bear. The *grizzly bear?* You are tolerated, like a child, encouraged to speak your piece; or you are handled with extreme care, like a madman. The real world is downtown; the rest is fantasy.

Some of us feel the wilderness mystique; some of us do not. This is true of most aspects of conservation affairs. In thoughtful, earnest discussion, many people will agree with one's arguments wholeheartedly on an intellectual basis, but then there develops a block. The emotional and philosophical jump from the centre of the universe to the perspective of the living world is simply too great, even for those who with the best of goodwill would readily attempt it. Our cultural traditions have done their work too well.

It is incomprehensible to many of us that there is any need to be concerned for the future of wild lands in Canada. Surely those wide-open spaces are almost endless. What this country needs, far from the discouragement of headlong northern development, is one hundred million more people, with population centres moving northward to take advantage of all that room. Trying to discuss the world demographic problem with the average Canadian is not a rewarding exercise. We could *never* lose the wilderness. There is so *much* of it!

There was once much wilderness in the United States.

But this is not the United States, we say. This is Canada, and the Canadian north is quite beyond the scope of even the most sophisti-

121

cated technology. It is too cold in winter; it is uninhabitable. This, of course, is preposterous. We have become extraordinarily blasé about men rocketing to the moon. There is no difficulty whatever in creating and sustaining artificial human environmental conditions. The fact is that we are despoiling the wilderness today and we will do it more intensively and to greater effect tomorrow.

If present trends continue, there seems no alternative to the gloomy prediction that the northern wilderness as we know it is doomed. Not tomorrow, perhaps, but the day after. It is quite possible that only the unthinkable event of world nuclear war can prevent it. Most thoughtful conservationists see every reason to expect that eventually all wild lands and wild creatures we see fit to spare will be behind fences. Whether we will be permitted to visit these places, under some strict regulation of our numbers, will be up to the governments of the day. It will be important to acknowledge at the outset that the blocks of wilderness we save must necessarily be large, so that their character will be unchanged. The farther north you go, the larger the blocks must be. There is a limited energy budget in the north because of the brief growing season, and it takes extremely great stretches of landscape to sustain the finely tuned ecosystem which has evolved there.

There is no doubt that in due time we will come to wilderness conservation. We have already started. The pity is that we are destroying natural areas faster than we can study them, and our decisions on types and locations of terrain to be preserved may not be as well informed as they might have been. But we will do it, after so much of the damage will have been done, and what we do will be so pathetically little and inadequate.

It is a bleak picture, but our record to date allows little optimism. It is obvious that we can do immeasurably better; the operative question is, *will* we? We have in abundance the resources of technology—our wit. We have in abundance the resources of the mind and spirit—our wisdom, so sadly underexploited. For me, the seat of the mischief is in the values and aspirations of contemporary society, which are to such a great extent the product of the Judaeo-Christian ethic. The ancient beliefs are firmly entrenched in us; they are epitomized in the icy egocentricity of the phrase *Terre des Hommes*.

This, to my mind, is the virus of the world illness. Its symptoms are visible on every hand in the colossal and generally unheeded waste of natural and human resources. It is not pleasant to contemplate a subsistence level of existence in a degraded urban environment, but, in the absence of ecologically oriented decisions, that will be the unhappy future of our species. Wilderness preservation is only part of the modern crisis, but when we lose the wilderness we will also lose our last tenuous contact with the real world from which we came. It is an ugly and frightening thought.

Wet bush, near Pointe au Baril, Ontario. Randy Saylor

Swamp, near Mississauga Lake, Peterborough County, Ontario. C. B. Cragg

Swamp, north of Pembroke, Ontario. J. Wallace

Camp, east end of Sifton Lake, Hanbury River, Northwest Territories. J. W. L. Goering

Waterfall, Timagami region, Ontario. Steve Moss

First Canyon, South Nahanni River, Northwest Territories. William D. Addison

Water-washed rock, Whiteshell Provincial Park, Manitoba. Robert R. Taylor

BLAIR FRASER

Ordeal and Triumph: The Trail of La Vérendrye

Last summer six middle-aged sedentary workers—three of us in our forties, three in their fifties, average age forty-eight—set out to retrace the steps of Pierre de La Vérendrye's men who discovered the fur-trade highway westward from Lake Superior.

We started as La Vérendrye did at the eight-mile portage around the rapids and falls at the foot of Pigeon River, just across the Ontario-Minnesota border. Grand Portage, it came to be called; in the heyday of the fur trade it was the meeting place each summer of 1,200 voyageurs who exchanged the winter harvest of furs from the interior for trade goods from Montreal.

We ended at Fort Frances, at the western end of Rainy Lake. La Vérendrye's men called it Fort St. Pierre; they wintered there in 1731, the first white men known to have traversed this chain of rivers and lakes over the height of land where the waters of the Gulf of St. Lawrence are parted from the waters of Hudson Bay.

Our Z-shaped route covered 266 miles—a couple of hours by bush plane or overnight by rail from Fort William. It took us eighteen days of strenuous but unhurried travel—242 miles by canoe and twenty-four on foot over sixty-five portages. They were days that began at four a.m., half an hour before sunrise, and ended when we crawled into sleeping bags at twilight, always tired and sometimes exhausted. They were also among the happiest days we've ever spent, days that gave us all a new awareness of Canada by bringing us into a kind of personal contact with Canada's past.

Not that this was a remarkable section, in the fur-trading days, of the great canoe route which began at Montreal and which Alexander Mackenzie and Simon Fraser finally extended all the way to the Pacific. It was commonplace then—so commonplace, in fact, that many of the early journals do not even describe it. What makes it remarkable now, a precious legacy that Canada and the United States are both trying to preserve intact, is the fact that this little stretch alone, of all the fur-trade highway, is still much as it was when Sir Alexander Mackenzie crossed it in his search for the western sea.

This essay is reprinted from *Maclean's Magazine* (October 1, 1954).

This is the wilderness, empty and lovely. Some stretches along these lakes and streams have never been logged; the pines that look down on the traveller today had already taken root when Pierre de La Vérendrye's men went through in the autumn of 1731. Here as nowhere else men of the twentieth century can feel the charm and some of the challenge the makers of Canada knew.

That's what the six of us went out to find, and we found it. We knew we would. This wasn't our first excursion together. The trip over the Grand Portage and beyond was the climax of a series that began four summers ago.

The first trip was conceived at a diplomatic cocktail party in Ottawa, of all unlikely places. Dr. Omond Solandt, then chairman of the Defence Research Board, and Eric Morse, national director of the Association of Canadian Clubs, challenged three visitors from various diplomatic missions to go on a canoe trip in the Canadian bush and see what this country is really like. It was a casual remark, but it was taken seriously.

Solandt used to be a forest ranger when he was in university, and though he hadn't seen much of the outdoors in the intervening twenty years he's as strong as an ox and knows his way around in the woods. Eric Morse is a fanatical outdoorsman who has been going on canoe trips for thirty years. I still don't know why they recruited me to be the third Canadian in the party—at that time I had never been on a canoe trip in my life.

Of the three non-Canadians on the original trip down the Gatineau Valley in 1951, two have since gone home. The only one still here is A. H. J. Lovink, the retired Netherlands Ambassador to Canada.

"I'm too old," he said when Eric Morse first invited him in 1951. "I'll be a drag on you fellows."

As it turned out Tony Lovink carried the biggest canoe and the heaviest pack and was the only one of the six who never complained of being tired. When I twisted an ankle on the Quetico River, during a 1953 trip through part of the same region we covered last summer, Tony carried me over the next portage piggyback. Before we set out in 1953 he had a physical checkup; the doctor said he had the heart, circulation and general physical equipment of a man of twenty-nine. Actually he celebrated his fifty-third birthday beside a campfire at Sturgeon Lake, on a rocky shelf now inscribed on our maps as Tony Island.

Lovink is now the most dedicated advocate of the Canadian wilderness you could find in all ten provinces. He spends a lot of time each winter giving illustrated lectures about it to Canadians; on a visit to Holland he gave the same lecture to Queen Juliana.

In this year's group the only other visitor from overseas was John Endemann, Deputy High Commissioner for South Africa. He was without question the bravest of the party.

John is only forty—"the boy," we called him—and there is little or no excess fat in his 195 pounds. But when he accepted to come along in place of Major-General Elliott Rodgers, General Officer Commanding at Winnipeg who couldn't come this year, John Endemann had never set foot in a canoe. The first time he ever carried one on his shoulders was the morning we started over the eight-mile Grand Portage—the portage that caused La Vérendrye's men to mutiny when they first tackled it 223 years ago. John made no complaint at the time but he admitted later that for the first three or four days he thought we were all crazy, and he the craziest of all for coming with us.

Sixth, oldest (fifty-five) and most valuable member of the 1954 party was Sigurd Olson of Ely, Minnesota, president of the National Parks Association of America, ecologist of the Izaak Walton League, a professional watchdog of the wilderness who spends much of his time lobbying to preserve it in Washington and in various state capitals.

Sig Olson has been woodsman for thirty years. He worked summers as a guide when he was at university, and ran a wilderness outfitting station for years after that. He knows the thousand-odd lakes of Quetico Provincial Park and the Superior National Forest as well as any man living. He can produce biscuits at a camp fireplace such as mother used to make from a reflector oven, or bannock almost as tasty from a greased frying pan. We called him "The Bourgeois," as the voyageurs of old called their employers, and we obeyed him faithfully in all things.

It was after a 200-mile trip last year under Olson's guidance that we got the idea of retracing La Vérendrye's footsteps. We were driving back to Fort William on the main highway that runs from Duluth. Just on the U.S. side of the border at Pigeon River the road crosses a wide grass-grown trail the Indians still use occasionally, a trail once famous and still known as Grand Portage.

As we drove across it the same thought occurred to several of us at once: Why not come out another summer, start at the Grand Portage and paddle over the old fur-trade highway to Fort Frances? We'd seen enough of the Quetico-Superior wilderness to know that on this section of the historic route we might see and feel and do some fraction of what the voyageur two centuries ago saw and felt and did.

We knew, of course, that it would be only a fraction.

A voyageur normally carried, on each trip over a portage, two oblong packages of goods weighing ninety pounds each; the 300-pound canoe itself was carried by the bowman and steersman, whose seniority entitled them to this relatively light and easy load. The heaviest of our aluminum canoes weighed only eighty-six pounds, and the packs we took over the Grand Portage were lighter than the canoes.

Each voyageur was expected to take eight packages over Grand Portage without extra pay—for each package above eight he got one Spanish dollar. That meant at least four trips for each man. Since furs from the interior were being brought down at the same time trade goods were sent up, a man often carried full loads each way. Sir Alexander Mackenzie, first explorer to cross the northern part of the continent to the Pacific, recalled one man who set off on the eight-mile portage with two ninety-pound packages and was back with two more in six hours.

It took us nearly six hours to go one way, with less than half his load. We decided our historical curiosity would be satisfied with only one carry over this first and longest portage, so we took only our three canoes—maximum weight eighty-six pounds—and three packs of about sixty pounds each. We would switch loads every ten minutes, and set them down for a rest every half hour. Meanwhile we'd hired three husky young Chippewas from the Grand Portage reservation to take over the rest of our nine packs.

We knew that going over the Grand Portage even once would be quite tough enough, and most of us had trained for the event. Solandt and Lovink spent two Saturdays paddling from Ottawa to the Island of Montreal, doing half the journey one week and driving down the following week to resume where they left off. Morse and I had made fifteen-mile day trips in the Gatineau Valley, one man carrying the canoe and the other a packsack weighted with Canada Year Books. Only John Endemann, the newcomer from South Africa who didn't know what he was getting into, was too busy to take part in these preliminary workouts.

We prepared for the journey in other ways too. All winter we read the records of voyageur times.

Most of La Vérendrye's journals have been lost, but we read what is left of them. We read Alexander Henry, the first and most engaging of the Yankee traders who flocked to the Northwest after New France fell, and his nephew and namesake who travelled over the same territory forty years later. We read David Thompson, the scholarly servant of two fur-trading companies, first explorer to carry a sextant through the Northwest, and respectfully mentioned in other journals of the time as "Mr. Astronomer Thompson." We read Sir Alexander Mackenzie and his clansman Roderick, who gave a precise description of the route with every portage named and paced off; Daniel Harmon, the priggish New Englander who was scandalized that voyageurs worked on the Sabbath but who promptly accepted a Chippewa chief's offer of his comely daughter as a "companion" during his stay in the woods; Dr. John J. Bigsby, who went as physician, draftsman and historian with the Boundary Survey Commission under "Mr. Astronomer Thompson" in 1823.

Eric Morse even took the trouble to copy out the passages from these old journals that refer specifically to our route. In his best Canadian Club manner he would read them to us in the evenings as we sat around the cooking fire consuming our ration of rye (three and a half ounces per man per day) and waiting for one of Sig Olson's pike chowders to cook.

It wasn't too difficult to imagine those old times when we sat down in the Grand Portage trading post, the night before we set out, to dine on a lake trout a Chippewa had caught for us three hours earlier. Grand Portage today is a somnolent little Indian village, far fallen since 1,200 voyageurs met there each summer, when the Montreal partners of the Northwest Company came out "wrapped in rich furs, their huge canoes freighted with every convenience and luxury." But the trading post is a faithful replica of the Nor'Westers' fort, rebuilt on the original site in the thirties as a relief project by the Roosevelt Administration. It's now operated on a concession basis for the U.S. Indian affairs bureau.

Around it as of old is a palisade of sharpened cedar posts seven or eight feet high, with bastions at each corner for the sentries. The archaic effect is somewhat marred by a modern steel-wire fence across the main gate, but inside the fort it's easy to slip back into the past. Stacked around are samples of Indian work, paddles and moccasins and fringed deerskin jackets; hanging from the ceiling is a twenty-seven-foot birch-bark canoe, the kind that once carried 3,000 pounds of goods and six or eight men from Lake Superior to the Red River.

We were standing under that canoe as we packed our own modest cargo—three packs for each of our three canoes. They were light this year, for we had learned the hard way what not to bring. Our sleeping bags weighed only three pounds apiece, a little skimpy for a really cool night but plenty if you bring along a suit of long underwear. Spare clothing was cut to a minimum. We each had a heavy shirt and blue jeans to keep off the flies on the portages, swimming trunks to wear in the canoes; light moccasins and spare socks to put on in the evenings when we got our canvas gym boots wet, as we did almost every day; a sweater for cool mornings and a peaked cap for sunny afternoons, and that was about it.

Sig Olson, who did all the cooking, had chosen and bought all the food, and we were amazed at the variety he could get in a minimum of weight and space. The six of us ate about twenty pounds of food a day; all of it was carried bone dry and most of it in light paper containers. Sig had cereals for breakfast, pancake and biscuit and muffin mixes for bread. He had dehydrated stews, blocks of corned beef, a side of bacon that lasted more than a week, and summer sausages that would have lasted until Doomsday. He had dried fruits, pudding powders, hard bar chocolate and three kinds of jam. We ate like kings, or like cormorants, at each of our fifty-four meals.

However, the packs felt heavy enough when we shouldered them and turned our backs on Lake Superior for the eight-mile carry to old Fort Charlotte (now not even a ruin, just a few grass-grown mounds). This long haul would take us past the rapids and falls that form the lower reaches of Pigeon River. Another fifty miles of stiff paddling, pulling and carrying upstream would take us to the height of land. From there on, the old journals assured us, it would be easy—by far the shortest, straightest, pleasantest route from the Great Lakes to the Great Plains.

At the outset even the explorers admitted the going was hard. Pierre de La Vérendrye went over it for the first time on August 26, 1731, and reported later that "all our people, in dismay at the length of the portage, three leagues, mutinied and loudly demanded that I should turn back."

The mutiny cheated La Vérendrye of a personal honour. He led the first party of white men to use this historic route, just as Col. John Hunt led the party that climbed Everest, but La Vérendrye like Hunt had to let someone else go first. His nephew La Jemeraye persuaded a few volunteers to press on, blaze the trail to Rainy Lake, and tap the rich fur trade of the interior. La Vérendrye had to winter on Lake Superior with the timorous mutineers, who would only go farther after La Jemeraye's band returned in the spring with a rich haul of beaver.

On a warm cloudy Thursday morning we understood how La Vérendrye's mutinous voyageurs felt.

There is no drinking water along the Grand Portage. For lunch, at which we were hosts to a million mosquitoes, we ate dry cheese sandwiches and chocolate bars—nothing liquid except an extra flask of whisky Tony Lovink had thoughtfully brought along. This was good, but wasn't exactly a thirst-quencher for men who had sweated several pints since breakfast.

The trail itself was in pretty good shape—apparently better than when Dr. Bigsby went over it in 1823, only twenty-one years after a new U.S. tariff had stopped the flow of Canadian goods, forced the Northwest Company to use a new all-Canadian route starting from Fort William, and had brought a sudden end to Grand Portage's days of glory. We waded knee-deep through buttercups and daisies, instead of the "briars and coppice" which Bigsby deplored. But in one respect the portage seemed unchanged.

"This is a labour," Sir Alexander Mackenzie remarked, "which cattle cannot conveniently perform in summer, as both horses and oxen have been tried without success."

We didn't stop at Fort Charlotte, as the traveller did in the old days. Then it was a comfortable post at the western end of Grand Portage; now we could find only a faint rectangle of low mounds which, in Sig Olson's opinion, marked the old foundations. Nothing else remained, though the swampy woods still swarmed with biting insects.

We pushed off as soon as we could and paddled upstream a couple of miles to the next portage, the quarter-mile or so around Partridge Falls.

"A hundred and twenty feet," Sir Alexander Mackenzie called this cataract, though Bigsby's survey commission found it was only forty-nine. In any case it was beautiful, and the rocky shelf at the top was comparatively free of insects. Even though the afternoon was less than half gone we made this our first campsite.

Next morning, three miles farther upstream, we found "La Prairie" or "the Meadow" which was a favourite stop for the fur traders. They too used to stop early on the first day and sample the liquor issued at Grand Portage. The Meadow, as the younger Alexander Henry remarked, provided "plenty of elbow room for the men's antics."

We had been puzzled to find this night stop so near the starting point at Fort Charlotte, but that day we found the reason. There wasn't another campsite on the whole rough length of the Pigeon River.

All day we sweated and strained upstream. We found and hacked our way through the overgrown Caribou Portage, but we passed by— unfortunately—the mile-and-a-half trail that would have led us into Fowl Lake. Instead we went on up the river, which was deceptively quiet at this point, but soon became again one shallow continuous rapid.

Altogether we had five and a half miles of rapids that day. We hauled the canoes up, wading anywhere from knee to waist deep in water so fast we could hardly keep our footing. Then we came upon a high dam in a gorge we couldn't get through—we had to find and blaze a portage of our own next morning. That was the hardest day of the whole trip. Even Solandt and Lovink, ordinarily as durable as a pair of bull moose, admitted they were all in when we made camp on a hill overlooking Fowl Lake.

We had a letdown waiting for us, too. On the Pigeon River we salved our weariness by reflection that this was wilderness seldom travelled since the fur traders stopped using it. On Fowl Lake, the first thing we saw was a shiny aluminum rowboat brought in by plane. As we paddled through next morning, planes came down every half-hour or so with fishing parties from Minnesota.

That was almost the last we saw of airborne trippers, though. Before the day was out we had reached the Superior National Forest, on the left shore of each lake as we paddled along the international boundary. There the United States maintains a roadless area and forbids aircraft to land. Every other nook and cranny of the continent is accessible by air but the U.S. protects this fragment of wilderness from hit-and-run visitations.

On the Canadian side, authorities refuse to let the U.S. fliers come down and circumvent American law. In spite of recommendations from conservation groups there is not yet a law to forbid flying in from Canadian points.

One reminder of the twentieth century we never quite escaped along the boundary route was the outboard motor. All the way from Gunflint Lake, just over the height of land, to big Basswood Lake that runs deep into Minnesota the portages are short and easy, the country is beautiful and the fishing is first class. Lots of people are willing to carry small boats and light motors over the portages here. Only in the heart of Quetico Provincial Park, north of Basswood Lake and off the shortest and easiest way west, could we count on silence all day.

We got to Basswood Lake, roughly halfway to Rainy Lake, in seven and a half days, about the normal time for a fur trading "brigade." Not that we were trying to race anybody living or dead. We were astonished to learn when we got home that we'd "failed to equal La Vérendrye's record." We didn't know what his record was, but we did know such comparisons are meaningless.

We, for example, had the advantage over La Vérendrye of knowing where we were going. We had no guides, and not even Sig Olson had been over all of the route before, but we did have large-scale maps with every headland shown and every portage marked. We were never once in doubt about where we were. We had a different advantage over later voyageurs who knew the route blindfolded: no cargo. They had to move a ton and a half of lading for each canoe across the thirty-five portages between Lake Superior and Basswood Lake. Our three canoes and nine packs could be taken over a short portage in one trip, and any portage in two.

On the rare occasions when voyageurs travelled light they really travelled fast. The younger Alexander Henry, waiting at Basswood Lake for a new canoe, noted in his diary: "At one o'clock Roderick Mackenzie arrived in a light canoe, two days out from Lac la Pluie (Rainy Lake) and expecting to reach Grand Portage early on the 29th"—i.e., in two more days, three and a half times as fast as we had come.

Travelling light then meant more than it does now. A man's food was Indian corn, one quart per man per day, boiled in lye to soften it and reheated on the voyage in a little bacon grease. Nothing else was provided, not even salt.

"This mode of victualling is essential to the trade," the elder Henry soberly remarked, "which, being pursued at great distances and in vessels so small as canoes, will not permit of any other food. If the men were to be supplied with bread and pork the canoes would not carry a sufficiency for six months, and the ordinary duration of the voyage [into the interior for a fur trading season] is not less than fourteen."

We had a variety of food that would have made a voyageur's eyes pop. We had two dozen fresh eggs and heaven knows how many powdered; we had six enormous steaks for the first night out, and a whole ham to be eaten in the first two or three days; with our various dehydrated meals and ready-mixed flours we had powdered milk and powdered cream and sugar and butter and jam. Also we kept a strict ration on our nine forty-ounce bottles of rye whisky, so we had to carry some all the way instead of drinking it up as the voyageurs did in one riotous binge.

When we set out from Basswood Lake for the second leg of the journey (after reprovisioning at a friend's summer place) our food weighed 180 pounds. We had to carry it over the long portage into Lake Kahshahpiwi—half a mile up a rocky mountainside, another half mile down again, with a soggy bog cupped in the middle at the summit. Anyone who has gone over this portage is entitled to membership in the Kahshahpiwi Club, an exclusive organization which offers its members no privileges whatever.

We cut north from Basswood Lake through the Kahshahpiwi chain to take in another famous old route to the west. This was the so-called "New Route" started at Fort William up the Kaministikwia River, the route the Northwest Company used after the U.S. tariff cut them off from Grand Portage in 1802. It was the path over which Sir George Simpson, the fabulous Hudson's Bay Company governor, carried his young bride 120 years ago. Also—and this attracted us most of all—it was the site of that most pathetic of Canadian enterprises, the Dawson Road.

Simon James Dawson, a Canadian Government civil engineer in the 1850's and 1860's, had the vision to see that if young Canada were going to claim sovereignty over the Northwest Territories she would have to find some way of getting to them without travelling through the U.S. He first surveyed the Northwest Company's route in 1857, and reported that a connected series of roads and canals, with steam barges on the larger lakes, was a perfectly feasible way of linking east and west.

Ottawa did nothing about the Dawson survey for more than a decade. Then half-heartedly, in 1868, work began on the Dawson Road westward from Port Arthur (then called Dawson's Landing) and eastward from the Red River Settlement. In fact, surveys for the Dawson Road there were a contributing cause of the Riel Rebellion in 1870.

The Red River Expedition, 400 regulars and 800 Canadian militia sent to put down the rebellion, finished the Dawson Road. It took them three months of miserable toil—when a reinforcement expedition went out later the same year it covered the distance in three weeks. Later the steam barge service was installed, the corduroy roads improved. No canals were dug, but dams, still standing, lengthened the navigable stretches on the lakes.

Dawson's Road is still visible along the Maligne River; the cedar logs are not quite rotted away. Sig Olson found and cached a rusty propeller from one of the steam barges.

They are relics of a failure. Dawson's Road was abandoned even before the C.P.R. went through and made it obsolete. The reason it failed was not the railway alone, though it was possible even then to go west by rail through the U.S. But as late as the 1870's, the cheapest way was still by canoe. Knowing that, and paddling down the same streams and lakes and over the same portages that still bear the same names, we felt close to the voyageurs.

Through the virgin wilderness of Quetico Park, and even in the western end of Rainy Lake, where half the islands have summer cottages and "No Trespassing" signs, we were able to cling to that sense of the living past. Finally, on the last nine miles of the trip, we met one of the commonest hazards of the voyageur, a big wind on a big lake. We rounded the point of a sheltering island and found ourselves in what must have been a thirty-mile gale.

How the laden canoes of old made out in such weather, we couldn't understand. Early chronicles note that with 3,000 pounds and a crew of six or eight in a canoe the gunwales sank within inches of the water. Our aluminum canoes were carrying no more than 500 pounds including our own weight, and they rode the three-foot rollers beautifully. But even they took water two or three times, and at every wave the bowman was drenched. The six of us looked and felt like drowned rats when we finally got to Fort Frances. It took us four hours to paddle the nine miles.

We hadn't more than set foot on the dock before civilization caught up with us. A family of recent immigrants from The Netherlands had been waiting to shake hands with Ambassador Lovink. Tony had been paddling bow and glistened with water all over. He had nothing on but a pair of spun-glass swimming trunks and a peaked cap with a gull's feather in it. He stepped ashore and greeted his compatriots with as much aplomb as if he were wearing striped pants and morning coat. Then he faded unobtrusively to the rear and came back with blue jeans and a shirt on.

We went into town after that, self-conscious about our twice-peeled noses and our black fingernails, and oppressively aware of the twentieth century. But we had one more experience to strengthen our feeling of contact with the past. In Fort Frances we talked to Captain William J. Wilson, then eighty-seven, who came out by canoe in 1881 as a boy of fourteen. He came to join his father, who had come out the year before and already had a bit of the farm where Wilson now lives in retirement.

"There were twenty-four of us in four canoes, men, women and children," Captain Wilson said. "I was counted a man—I was nearly fourteen, and paddled bow all the way. We went by train from Port Arthur to the Savanne River (about fifty miles inland) and paddled from there to Fort Frances in eleven days."

What did they have to eat?

"Flour, salt pork and tea. We used to make a kind of bread each night, and we caught some fish and rabbits."

Did they have tents?

"No, you slept wherever you could find a flat spot. Two blankets apiece."

What did they do about the mosquitoes and black flies?

"Just let 'em bite."

Did they have their goods done up in packs for the portages?

"It was a jumble—everything in a heap. I remember one man had a hive of bees and several had ducks and hens."

That was the only way to get to Fort Frances through Canadian territory for nearly twenty more years—until near the turn of the

139

century when Mackenzie and Mann ran a line from Port Arthur to Rainy Lake, even though the C.P.R. had gone through to Winnipeg in the early eighties.

As we drove back to the hotel after talking to the eighty-seven-year-old pioneer, I asked newcomer John Endemann the question I hadn't dared put to him before: "Are you glad you came? Was it worthwhile?"

His answer took a weight off my conscience. "I wouldn't have missed it for anything," he said. "It was hard, very hard at times, but it was good. You know, in the foreign service we like to get to know the countries to which we are posted. I feel I have learned something of Canada that I couldn't have learned any other way."

He was absolutely right, of course, but the sad fact is that too few Canadians learn it either.

Boreal forest in morning mist, Caliper Lake, Ontario. Robert R. Taylor

Whooping crane breeding habitat, Wood Buffalo National Park, Alberta. Dalton Muir–National Parks

143

Glacial erratic boulders on bedrock, near Kenora, Ontario. Robert R. Taylor

Glacial erratics, near Peggy's Cove, Nova Scotia. Dalton Muir

Deadfalls in swamp, near Chapleau, Ontario. Robert W. Barnett

Great blue heron rookery, Basswood Lake, Quetico Provincial Park, Ontario. Bruce Litteljohn

Northern Ontario timber wolf. William C. Mason

R. YORKE EDWARDS

The Proof of Wildness: Where Caribou Still Stand

The north woods can be a pleasant place in summer. Increasing numbers of Canadians know this to be true because they have been there. But the north is no paradise. If it were, more people would be living there. The north has one basic flaw: winter dominates its year, and severely limits the variety and abundance of its living things.

Animal abundance usually reflects the richness of the land. By world standards the north has a poor showing of animal species, and those animals that do occur need much space in which to find a living. The boreal forest does not grow in a rich land, for the glaciers carried off much of the soil. On the Canadian Shield, which covers a large part of Canada, the hard rocks have not produced much new soil; that which is present is biologically poor; and long, cold winters further limit the kinds of life that can live on what soil there is.

In spite of the harshness of the northern landscapes and of the problems that the animals there must surmount, there is an abundance of animal life to see. In summer the land is alive with birds, some of them vivid with colours appropriate to the tropics. A bewildering variety of small creatures can enliven the night. Large and glamorous species known well to the *coureurs de bois* still live out their lives only a short canoe trip away from smog and traffic jams and life-by-the-clock. Just north of most Canadians, wolves still rumble out deep throaty howls in the night; mink still hunt the shores of lakes with fierce intensity; beaver still swim up the path of the moon; and caribou still stand in the mists of morning to test the air for scented news.

Cold is the north's burden. Most people, and most birds, in the north are part-time users, enjoying the summer but retreating from winter. Most other life is much less mobile, and is forced into year-round residence. Among these residents are the most interesting northern animals, for their being there at all is proof that their kind has solved the problems of year-round survival in a cold, demanding land. The main hazards that these residents must face are the long and deadly winters. By contrast, summer survival is mainly a simple matter of luck with predators and disease.

Moose, the world's largest deer, are famous residents of northern forests. A brief look at their survival problems suggests the sorts of challenge that a northern winter offers. Remember, however, that while moose are confronted by typical northern problems, they often solve them in ways peculiar to moose. Each kind of animal lives the details of life in its own way.

The north may seem warm enough to the summer visitor, but the balmy time of year in the boreal forest is only a few months, between the last frosts of June and the first frosts of September. Cold and some of its side effects are the main causes of moose hard times. Like most animals, they also face the hazards of accidents, predators, parasites and disease, but given luck and good food these are not usually serious problems until old age changes the odds.

Moose are made from water and the branches and leaves of plants, most of them trees and shrubs. This is what all moose are made of. A moose is a self-propelled machine for processing a more or less continuous flow of plant materials. The long mobile lip that gives the distinctive moose profile is designed to grasp twigs and small branches, then to pass them to rows of large grinding teeth set in powerful jaws. Cut and ground to bits and slivers, then mixed with water and other chemicals, the branches are transported along yards and yards of the intestinal pipeline that fills much of the moose's body. Along this pipeline nutritious parts are extracted to build and repair the moose-machine, and to be used as fuel to power it.

Each day a moose takes forty to sixty pounds of its environment into its body as food. This large amount is necessary because the food is not very nutritious, partly the result of branches not being very nutritious anywhere, and partly because low temperatures in cold climates limit the rate and extent of biological processes, hence limit the quality of the moose's living food. With luck, all goes well enough for moose in summer; the energy intake usually is in excess of needs. The surplus is stored as fat until needed. Then comes winter. The cold, sometimes well below zero for weeks, causes a greatly increased loss of body heat to the environment. As a result, more energy is needed to maintain body temperature. But this is only part of the problem. Because of the cold, precipitation falls in solid form and soon lies deep on the ground. This hinders walking while moose gather their daily loads of plants, and the deeper the snow gets the more energy must be spent to collect the food required. A dangerous situation develops if the animals use energy faster in collecting food than they take it in with the food collected. As long as fat reserves set aside in summer can pay the debt, all is well, but a prolonged energy drain soon has the animals near starvation, and thus especially vulnerable to predators, disease, and accidents. Starvation itself is inevitable unless conditions improve. Notice especially that this is starvation on full stomachs. There need be no lack of food, although there may be poor access to it because of snow.

Most moose, like most northern animals perhaps, die in winter. Since weather influences whole regions at once, it affects many animals at once. In some years, winter kills large numbers of moose—and deer as well—across miles of the northern landscape. It can be a common experience to find their remains in the woods the next summer. In these years there is usually much nonsense in the press about the great slaughter by wolves. The truth, however, is in the remains of the dead animals. A long bone from a leg contains marrow that has the facts. If the marrow is red and has no solid fat, starvation was the main cause of death.

Deer in northern forests face problems similar to those of moose. One major difference in deer, however, is their shorter legs; they flounder in snow that is still not too deep for the long legs of moose. Deer partly solve this problem by assembling in "yards." These are simply areas with relatively good food and relatively light snow where, because there is a concentration of deer, energy is conserved by doing part of the daily travelling on trails already beaten down by others.

Red squirrels solve the energy problem by collecting seeds in the autumn. Seeds are usually especially good for supplying energy, and when they are collected beforehand there is no snow problem connected with gathering enough food in winter.

Black bears do the same thing, but instead of storing energy for winter in the form of a seed hoard, they store it in the form of fat. They then find shelter, turn down the processes of life to reduce the consumption of energy, and doze away the winter in a sort of half-hibernation. True hibernators, like chipmunks and woodchucks, pick a burrow in the warm earth, slow the metabolism so the spark of life is barely aglow, and pass the winter in deathlike unconsciousness. In this way they get maximum living time from their stored fat.

The storing of food, whether as seeds or as fat, may be the best way to survive the winter, but cold can still kill squirrels and bears. Some years are lean years in the north woods, even in summer, when seeds are scarce or the berry crops fail. The result for the winter sleepers can be too little excess energy accumulated by winter to keep the motor of life running until spring.

Birds and bats which live on active insects can find no food in a northern winter. Being highly mobile, they simply avoid winter by going to where there is none, and therefore to where there are insects. Many of the insectivores are quick, active creatures living at a fast metabolic pace, and they burn up energy faster than do most animals. Many would starve if without food for a long night. For this reason night can be a problem for the birds; bats face the same problem in the day. Lengthening nights in August and September force many birds to leave the north when insects are still abundant. There are simply too few daylight hours to take in enough fuel to keep life going through the long, cool nights. The simplest solution is to retreat to shorter nights. Bats solve their problem in another way. After hanging themselves up for the day, to rest, they slow down their metabolic rate and enter a brief bit of hibernation-like sleep. While this makes them slow to react to a daylight crisis, it does prevent starvation as they rest.

Northern animals have many ways to cope with cold, snow and a scanty diet. Since their great challenges are in winter, that is when there is the most drama in their lives. Summer, on the other hand, is a time to multiply and to gather strength for the next winter. In summer when the north is warm, and usually there is an abundance of food, the vacationer will not think much of winter, and probably will not think at all about winter in the lives of the other animals enjoying summer with him. Perhaps this is as it should be. Summer is for lazy enjoyment, and it is alive with things to be looked at, and wondered at, in their summer settings. In most of the north, the best way to see the most is from a canoe.

A canoe is a magic thing, and it works its greatest magic on animals. Creatures that would not let a walking man within half a mile will let a man in a canoe close enough to hear their breathing. If the wind is right, a man is no longer a man in a carefully handled canoe.

With attention to silence and a habit of alertness, the voyageur cannot miss observing shy creatures doing interesting things. Shorelines and riverbanks are highways for large mammals, hence are good places to see deer and bears, moose, and perhaps a wolf. Weedy shallows attract deer and moose to feed. Some animals are always water-oriented, like beavers and ospreys, mink and kingfishers. Dull days and twilight are the best times to see mammals. On hot, still days even the daylight creatures are inactive. The siesta is not only a Spanish idea. Try it—with the rest of nature—when in canoe country.

For poetry of motion and *joie de vivre* the northern champions are otters. Family groups are the rule with fun and play their main concern when they are not hunting. They swim with ease and power, at home enough in water to be quite seal-like in many movements and attitudes. Their surges after fish are impressive shows of aquatic ability as they drive their prey into shallows or the crevices of rocky shores. When surprised in a narrow place they may show more curiosity than fear. They rise up vertically from the water for better views, and there is so much snorting and blowing among them that it would be difficult to pass them unnoticed.

Beaver are interesting enough, but they have been overrated. They are usually dull fellows that somehow manage to make felling trees, digging canals and damming rivers quite unspectacular to watch. At the same time there can be no denying their impressive works. The stump of a large tree felled by beaver makes my teeth ache as I look at it, and several hundred yards of dam curving across a valley is a major achievement by whatever means. Beavers are large and strong and programmed for some unusual activities, but there the compliments must end. In spite of many enthusiastic accounts of beaver intelligence, this is a typical rodent spending much of its life chewing or doing nothing at all. But still the beaver is a good symbol for much of Canada. The shining ripples from a beaver swimming in the twilight are worth special vigils to see. The slap of a beaver tail on the water may be an alarm to other beavers, but to the passing voyageur it is the reassurance that his favourite waterways are still wild and clean.

The north is moose country, and in late summer some moose take to the water for most of their feeding. The perfect way to watch them is from a canoe. They eat aquatic plants, plunging the head underwater to reach them, raising the head to chew and swallow. A cautious approach, with gentle paddling that coincides with the underwater plunges, makes close inspection fairly easy. But beware, for a moose is large and powerful. Sudden alarm can result in explosive action, and if it feels trapped in any way, a cornered moose will not give time for a graceful retreat.

White-tailed deer are not so aquatic in their summer feeding, but occasionally the situation is right for using canoe magic. One still morning I edged the bow of my canoe to within three feet of a doe feeding in shallow water. I was mystified at my success and concluded that she was either blind, or someone's pet. When I raised my arm quickly to test my theory the poor deer responded violently. She darted shoreward in panic-stricken retreat, to run headlong into a large boulder. After running into the rock a second time fully as energetically as the first, she changed direction enough to run for the forest. With the bow of my canoe only a few feet away, she had not known that I was a man.

The birds seen from canoes are mainly large ones, but one exception is the tree swallow. These small birds are at home on the wing where their constant aerobatics are in reality a constant war on the abundance of insects. This is the plain and graceful swallow most common over northern waters, and is perhaps the wildlife species seen most often by the water traveller in the north woods.

The far views available from lakes are ideal for seeing large, soaring birds. Among several hawks seen in the north, the osprey is the hunter of fish. This is the bird that, along with the bald eagle, builds bulky nests by rivers and lakes that become famous landmarks along many canoe routes. There is good entertainment in watching a hunting osprey as it plunges into the water from high above it. After witnessing hundreds of dives, I am impressed at how seldom they catch fish.

Not all soaring birds are hawks. The clown of the north—the raven —soars hawk-like over much of wild Canada. Ravens are often in pairs that commonly roll and tumble together in impressive shows of aerial skill, while their endlessly variable calls, some mellow, some harsh, carry far across the quiet land. The voyageur who has not taken the time to enjoy ravens, or who has somehow confused them with mere crows, has been missing the greatest feathered personality in the north.

Canoeing in canoe country is different things to different people. Some are content just to let the simple life sink in. Others are in love with the northern scene, but take it in as a total picture with little concern for its parts. These satisfactions are real, and valuable, and worth pursuing. But the people who get the most from northern experiences are those who look forward each summer to greeting whisky jacks, to hearing whitethroats sing, or to seeing more of dragonflies hawking over lily pads. Here as elsewhere production is related to input. In this case a little input of naming things and delving into their roles in life can produce a lifetime of pleasure from the details of northern scenes. All it takes is a little curiosity and the habit of solving small mysteries.

Daylight should not get all the attention from voyagers; darkness offers a special kind of entertainment. Most nights under canvas are intervals of oblivion between strenuous days, but there are sleepless times when the nights seem filled with life. An hour spent enjoying the show can be worth remembering. It is entertainment in sound. Ripples lapping wetly on the shore, and the wind—real music if the trees above are pines—give soothing background sound. These alone may be enough to communicate the fact of a wild place in a great solitude. But there can be other sounds, some of them very Canadian, a few even exciting if shivers in the back are any indication.

On many nights there are thumps and shufflings suggesting night visitors. Most remain mysterious. In the dead of night little sounds suggest large bears or whole herds of deer, but most are tricks of the wind or the rustlings of shy little creatures like snowshoe rabbits or flying squirrels. Occasionally big noises prove to have very small origins, as when the cold feet of a deer mouse flit across one's forehead. In a careless camp, however, small sounds can mean trouble outside if food has lured in a bear, or if a porcupine has found a sweaty axe-handle to chew. All of these are the muffled sounds of most nights, half imagined and seldom identified, but not all dwellers of the north woods are shy and cautious and uncommunicative. Some specialize in sound.

The tenderfoot on his first venture into lake country soon hears loons, and for the rest of his life will never forget them. Nothing else is like them. Their sounds are wild and shrill and eerie with a touch of madness, heard often enough to be known to every northern traveller, yet seldom enough to make every sustained concert a memorable event. To lie awake with the music of loons can be to glimpse in essence the lure of the north woods. Both loon and land are free and untamed, alive, unique and harsh. Anyone who has canoed the north or walked its trails will go suddenly thoughtful at the sound of loons. The calls have magic, even from a record player deep in a southern city. It is there, perhaps, that the magic works its best. The call of a loon is then the call of the land that makes them.

Loon sounds command attention for they strike chords that capture the mind and send shivers up the back. They are pure primitive sound. Wolf music is different. Shivers released by wolves are probably direct descendants of those that shook cavemen huddled in ice-age caves. Healthy wolves do not attack people, not now anyway, but the modern shiver is partly old fear, and is mixed I suspect with a response—as in the loon—to the sound itself. Wolf howls are low and full with all the loneliness that canine howls express. Some wolf voices are so low that vibrations seem as much felt on the skin as heard by the ear. Wolf sounds are easily within range of a man's voice. A little practice at howling can qualify a man to join wolves in duets, or to participate in the choral sessions of packs. He can even begin a wolfish song that nearby wolves will join.

In whippoorwill country the night show can be dominated by continuous monotonous comments on poor Will. Sometimes it helps to count these calls instead of sheep when insomnia threatens, but this has its hazards. On one camping trip, counting whippoorwill calls developed into a contest when we began counting the calls repeated in series without pause. It was mildly entertaining, wondering when the world's record was going to fall. The longest run was 286, a record established only after much enforced insomnia.

Some sounds in the night can remain mysteries for years. I first heard the rhythmic crunching sounds in a cabin where they seemed to come from the woodpile. I heard them again at irregular intervals from a dead spruce, from some fallen timber, then in a cabin again but this time from the wall. I finally learned that these are the feeding noises of a wood borer munching its way through dry wood. The animal involved is a plump white worm or grub that completes the larval stage to become a free-flying long-horned beetle. There are many kinds of these Cerambycids, a group of beetles identified as adults by unusually long thin antennae that woodsmen have labelled "long horns."

Not all sounds in the night are heard best from bed. It is more exciting sometimes to be mobile and able to strain the eyes into the night. My favourite vantage point is a canoe on familiar water, for the acoustics there are especially good. One night spent quiet and listening on a lake in Algonquin Park was especially rewarding. I was studying beaver that summer and was out to spy on their night life. The moon was full and the night became memorable for its show of northern lights. But the animals were impressive too. I found beaver active. Occasionally I drifted too close in the gloom, and there was a warning crash of broad tail on resisting water that temporarily ended the show. They were feeding. I could hear them chewing and to my surprise they were eating spruce, for I could smell it on the damp air. While I concentrated on beaver, a fox yapped, soprano, from the south shore. Great blue herons flew about in the night, squawking. The usual bullfrog chorus waxed and waned erratically. Bats darted about, fleeting forms sensed in the eerie light of rising mists aglow with moonlight and the light of the aurora. A wolf, bass and gruff, howled from the far shore. And, as on most nights, there were whippoorwills, nighthawks and deer splashing and snorting explosively from the shallows.

Try a bit of lethargic night canoeing for a new experience. It is one that might be memorable as the first time you felt yourself a part of a wild place instead of just a spectator looking in. And in a place that you know well, you may find that you still have much to learn.

In the wild and chaotic landscape of British Columbia there are two mountains that I know well. Both are low as mountains go, with long flat tops. In each case, the flat lands are just high enough to be above timberline, so each mountain is crowned by miles of open meadows with slopes and cliffs at their edges. Fir forest invades the tundra only in sheltered places.

On both mountains the same kinds of trees struggle up to treeline; the same sort of avalanche lily carpets the ground in spring; the same species of hoary marmot whistles at passers-by from strongholds in the rocks. Both mountains have far views on all sides because both tops are on the roof of the world. But similar as they are, the two mountains are different in one important way. One still has grizzly bears. The other has none. The difference is profound. One mountain is complete, still having its one most highly evolved, most easily destroyed part. The other lost its grizzlies decades ago and thereby became, by amputation, incomplete. To walk on a mountain that has grizzly bears is to walk where man has not yet smashed the biological harmony. To walk there is also a small adventure. The slight element of danger sharpens the wit and tunes the senses. Just the footfall of a ptarmigan or the snort of a deer can release adrenalin and raise the hackles. Grizzly country is a pleasant experience because it makes one feel uncommonly alive. When mountains have no grizzlies, much of the zest has gone from the landscape.

Not all of Canada has grizzly bears, but every wild part has its famous animals, its glamour species that by their presence indicate a wild landscape of high quality. That is precisely what these animals are—indicators. Each animal indicates, simply by its successful residence, not only the special kind of countryside that will provide the peculiar needs of that animal, but also that man has not yet lowered the wildness of that place to the point where that delicate indicator can no longer exist. Here I am thinking not only of the Canadian Shield with its wolves and woodland caribou, its wolverines and otters, but of the rest of Canada as well with its polar bears and walruses, seals and musk oxen, bighorn sheep and mountain caribou, ferruginous hawks and pronghorn antelopes, badgers and grey whales. With more sorrow, I am thinking also of passenger pigeons and great auks, of Canada's sea otters, and of those following close behind them, like whooping cranes, peregrine falcons, prairie falcons and bald eagles.

Much of Canada is still wild country, and much of that wildness is the result of the land having severe limitations for traditional human use. By our medieval standards for measuring the worth of land, this fact is a burden on Canada. From any reasonably imaginative look forward, however, its present limitation assures these lands of a unique and valuable future. In a world destined to swarm with people, there is no doubt whatever that among the scarcest and most valuable commodities of the next century will be clean water, clean air, space, solitude, freedom and wildness. Where there is wildness, the other five will be assured. Then, as now, the proof of real wildness will be whether moose still bob for plants along the shores of lakes; whether otters still play tag in the rivers; and whether bull caribou still stand curiously on wild shores watching solitary canoes cross lonely lakes. The future market is assured. The only fact in doubt is whether we can maintain the quality of the product.

Muskoxen, Cornwallis Island, Northwest Territories. Fred Bruemmer

Approximately 4,000 Barren Ground caribou, Bathurst Inlet, Northwest Territories. William I. Campbell

159

Polar bears, west coast of Hudson Bay, Northwest Territories. Fred Bruemmer

Walrus on small island, northern Hudson Bay. Fred Bruemmer

Break-up ice, Thelon River, Northwest Territories. Robert R. Taylor

Iceberg and pack ice off Baffin Island, Northwest Territories. Fred Bruemmer

Eskimo from Ellesmere Island crosses Jones Sound at night, Northwest Territories. Fred Bruemmer

BRUCE WEST

The Wilderness Breed: An Affectionate Memoir

Although no student of the Bible I know has ever been able to find it for me, my late Grandmother Nancy West used to claim that somewhere in the Good Book it was predicted that the world would grow "wiser, but weaker."

She was the widow of a Muskoka lumberjack she married at the age of sixteen, and her interpretation of this alleged prophecy was that as people learned more, with each succeeding generation, there was a corresponding drop in their ability to accomplish such worthwhile tasks as carrying a sack of flour for thirty miles or bucksawing a cord of wood as a mild workout before dinner.

In her late eighties she liked to smoke an occasional cigarette (a habit I'm afraid I taught her when she was an impressionable youngster in her seventies) and read Chums Annual, a great thick book for boys, full of hair-raising tales of adventure in the distant outposts of what was then a vast and powerful British Empire. Although she was impressed with some of the fictitious exploits of the young men described in Chums, she had certain reservations about the flesh-and-blood generation then growing up in the small Muskoka town where I was born.

It was a lumbering town, mainly, with three mills running night and day. Great log booms were towed down the lakes each summer from the river mouths where the sticks of timber had been collected at the sorting jacks after the spring drive. Old river-drivers usually ended up crippled with rheumatism because, no matter what kind of man you are, the human body is just not capable of being submerged to the waist in near-freezing water every other day of every spring, year after year, without damage. Many, of course, never got to be rheumatic old men because they were swept away while wrestling log jams in some swollen rapids; and wherever there was a rafting gang with a mouth-organ player there could be heard sad songs about the brave river-driving boys who never returned to their fair young maidens.

Many of the most memorable wilderness characters I have met were those I knew when I was a youngster. There don't seem to be as many of their breed around now, but that may be a finding that exists, like beauty and so many other things, only in the eyes and the memory of the beholder. The places and the people we encountered in youth always look bigger in memory. The hills look higher and the rivers wider and the men taller and braver. That's why you can never go back, even when you try, because so much has shrunk and it's perhaps better to leave it alone, there in your memory, where you can enjoy it in all its large dimensions and bold, bright colours, as it was.

Yet, even making allowance for the special light that bathes the people and events of the younger days of a man's life, it still sometimes seems to me that we are indeed becoming wiser but, at least physically, weaker, as humanity learns to exert greater control over its environment and to lessen the drudgery and physical hardships with which nature once so sternly tried those who faced our earlier frontiers. Once, in a lumber camp years ago, I saw several men squatting about on the floor while a companion sat on the side of his bunk with a month-old weekly newspaper. He read it aloud to them, by the light of an overhanging lantern, and the men around him hung on his every word, because there in the silence of the woods there was nothing more interesting for them to listen to. On a winter's night, as you crunched out of the smelly bunkhouse into the sharp and welcome freshness of the frosty winter air, it was so still you could hear your own pulse beating.

Recently, in a lumber camp bunkhouse in Northern Ontario, I saw loggers sprawled comfortably on their cots as they casually watched Dean Martin on a portable television set. Parked outside were late-model automobiles, ready to whisk their owners into town for a Saturday night in the comparatively bright lights. I saw a pulpwood camp where lunches were taken to the workers in the bush every noon in a special cafeteria truck, stocked with hot meat and potatoes and plenty of steaming gravy for all.

Modern ingenuity has made life in the wilderness more pleasant for many, but it has also brought about a certain uniformity of thought and action and outlook which is perhaps the wrong atmosphere in which to produce the kind of individuals found in our nation's wilderness folklore. It has always been a puzzle to me, in fact, which came first; did the man come to the wilderness because he was a certain rare kind of individual or did the wilderness produce him out of fairly ordinary stock? Or was it a combination of both, of a certain kind of man and a certain kind of life meeting there in some remote and lonely place to create what we call a backwoods *character?*

Old Bill Young, who used to come to town at least once a month for a little sociable drinking, was a fire ranger. He had a drooping white moustache that was wild and unruly and the skin along the bottoms of his eyes sagged in such a way that there was always some red showing, even when he hadn't been drinking. He'd broken a leg in the bush when a tree fell on it many years before and he had set the limb himself. He proudly claimed that when he'd finished the job there were enough bits of bone left over to feed the sparrows all winter and that leg did have a remarkable bow in it, contributing a great deal to Old Bill Young's generally gnarled appearance.

It was said that Old Bill Young hardly ever bothered to wear socks, except in the coldest days of winter, and it did seem he was of such toughness that he'd last forever, like the rocky Muskoka hills overlooking the Big East River. But one month Old Bill Young didn't come into town and the word got around that he had died back there in the forest near Algonquin Park where he'd spent all his life. We missed him when he didn't come to town anymore, with his bowed leg and his fierce moustache and his red-rimmed eyes, like those of an untamed old St. Bernard who preferred the company of the wolves to that of men.

The first time I ever met Chester Nichol was in the lobby of the Dominion Hotel. He was wearing a fancy oilcloth tie on his red checkered shirt and this cravat was as shiny as the top of Chester's head, which was so bare of hair it fairly glittered. Chester lived in Algonquin Park, where he did odd jobs for various employers and possibly poached a mink or two when the rangers weren't looking. He lived in a tiny shack on the shore of Cache Lake. To tell the truth, it wasn't the kind of abode you might find featured in *Good Housekeeping* magazine. It was more like a groundhog den and once when I dropped in to visit Chester there was something hanging over the back of his stove that was so black and greasy I thought for a moment he was brazenly and openly curing an illegal beaver hide. But it turned out to be only his tea towel.

Chester usually wore his hat both inside and outside his house, but one day he startled the residents of Algonquin Park by appearing among them not only hatless but also sporting a fine auburn head of hair where once there had been only that dazzling expanse of skin. It seems that Chester, in his spare time, of which he had a great deal, had decided to fashion a toupee out of deer hide, with all the hair left on. Although it added a certain amount of dash to his appearance, Chester wore this homemade wig only when the mood happened to strike him. For what might be called everyday wear, he still preferred his stained and battered hat, and there were those who claimed he slept in it.

Among Chester's many accomplishments, such as making deerskin toupees, digging post holes, poaching and engaging in rough carpentry, one of the greatest was wine-making. He loved to experiment with whatever materials he happened to have on hand. One batch might consist mainly of potato rinds, yeast and raisins while another might utilize more refined ingredients, such as prunes, canned peaches and dried apples.

One day, after concocting a particularly complex mixture, containing almost everything in his cabin that was not definitely labelled poisonous, he ran into Norman Paget, who was then one of the owners of Highland Inn. He announced to Norman that a batch of twelve bottles was now sufficiently aged and ready for consumption and invited him to drop over that night to help him sample what promised to be a most memorable vintage.

When Norman knocked that evening on the door of Chester's cabin, he heard a shuffle inside and then watched the light in the window grow brighter when Chester turned up the wick of his lamp, as was his custom before opening the door at night. Inside, after welcoming Norman, Chester waved proudly to the rows of tightly corked bottles lined up on his table in the lamplight.

He then proceeded, without delay, to the business of the evening. As he pulled the cork on the first bottle, there was a loud report and a great hissing as the wine spewed out like the stream from a high-pressure fire hose. When the shower of wine subsided, there was hardly a drop left in the bottle. The next bottle exploded with such force that it leaped right out of Chester's hands and went spinning madly across the floor of his shack. Bottle after bottle behaved in the same unruly manner as the corks were pulled, until finally Chester, his guest, and the whole interior of his cabin were heavily dripping with wine. With only two unopened bottles left, not enough wine had yet been salvaged to provide a single drink. But Chester was undismayed.

"Normie," said he happily, as he reached for bottle Number Eleven, "this is shore as hell goin' to be great wine, if we ever get 'er cornered!" They finally did, to the extent of half a glass apiece.

Chester died in a home for the aged a few years ago, where he spent his last days after being found sick and unable to look after himself in his dark little cabin on the shore of Cache Lake. You are unlikely to find such men as Chester Nichol or Old Bill Young around Algonquin Park anymore.

Nor the like of Abe McCann, for that matter. Abe wasn't exactly *in* Algonquin Park, a fine geographical distinction which Abe was careful to point out at every opportunity, particularly if there was a game warden within earshot. But the shack from which he tended his trap lines was situated on the very edge of the park, so close that in a heavy blizzard—or maybe a dark night—a man could easily lose his way and stray within the borders of this preserve while making his sets for beaver or mink.

When Abe started trapping on the edge of the park, Algonquin was patrolled by rangers on foot, or in canoes when the water was open. In winter they carried out their surveillance of the park borders using dog teams and sleds. It wasn't difficult for a really good poacher to slip in and out of the park without being detected. There was a cleared strip that ran around the entire border of the park and the trick was to cross this in winter without leaving telltale tracks which could be followed by a ranger on patrol.

At least one poacher managed to do this by making a pair of stilts with the feet carved in the shape of deer hooves. Walking across the boundary strip on his stilts, he carried his snowshoes on his back. Once in the cover of the forest, he simply cached his stilts and put on his snowshoes for the rest of his journey.

But when Frank A. MacDougall became the first flying Superintendent of Algonquin Park, the era of easy poaching ended. Day after day he soared and circled over his nearly 3,000-square-mile domain in an open-cockpit Fairchild biplane. Not much missed his eagle's eye, especially in winter, when a set of snowshoe tracks can be plainly seen, like a string of beads, winding across the lake ice and clearings.

Abe McCann considered the aerial inspection trips a personal affront and often sounded off loudly to his cronies in Huntsville against the essential evil of any government that would stoop to such things. But the coming of the airplane to Algonquin Park did scare the hell out of Abe, as it did every trapper who had formerly treated in rather casual fashion the line that marked the border of the great preserve.

Abe McCann was a giant of a man, with a booming voice to match his powerful physique. We always respected him because of the local legend about his great sorrow. When he was a young man he had farmed a few acres he had laboriously cleared in the bush near Oxtongue Lake. One winter Abe's wife was approaching her time to have their first child and he was making plans to take her into Huntsville, where she could receive proper care, because there were no neighbours close by.

But Abe's wife began to feel her labour pains coming on one stormy February night, many days before she had expected them. Abe's only horse was sick in the stable and, when he lit a lantern and went out through the blizzard to look at the animal, he realized it could never haul them to town. Returning to his little house, he anxiously watched as his wife's pains grew sharper and closer. At last, in desperation, he bundled her in blankets and carried her out to the cutter, where he made her as comfortable as he could. Then, climbing between the shafts and taking them up in his own great hands, he hauled that cutter through the snow drifts the whole sixteen miles to Huntsville.

It was hours before he reached the town and the story was that when he did get there, through the bitter cold and blizzard of that awful night, both his young wife and his first child were dead.

When I first met big Jack McCurdy he was running a commercial whitefish camp on the shore of Onaman Lake near Geraldton, Ontario. His crew netted the fish through holes in the ice during the winter months and it was beastly cold out there in the wind on a forty-below-zero day. Jack kept a couple of bottles of rum on the cookhouse table, along with the ketchup and the H.P. sauce. When one of his men felt the need of it he simply came in, poured out half a glass of grog, downed it in one gulp, and went back out to work on the ice. Jack's crew never found the rum bottle empty.

Before he got into the commercial fishing business, Jack McCurdy had been one of the leading guides on the famed trout waters of the Nipigon River. On a trip to Canada in the 1920's, Edward, Prince of Wales, was taken up to the Nipigon on a fishing trip. McCurdy was in charge of the party, which camped out during part of the expedition.

Naturally, the Prince was accompanied by a sizeable retinue of English aides and Scotland Yard men. One evening His Royal Highness decided he'd like to go for a swim in the Nipigon. The spot was full of dangerous-looking eddies and the members of the Prince's party were alarmed. They tried to talk the Prince out of it, but he was a young man with a mind of his own in such matters. Finally, they suggested a compromise. Perhaps it might be all right for him to go swimming if the Prince allowed a line to be tied to his waist, which could then be held by one of the guides in a canoe?

It seems the Prince became really indignant at the suggestion he should be dangled from a line while swimming, after the undignified fashion of a child being dunked at the end of a rope while paddling in a pond. Try as they would, the anxious guardians of His Royal Highness could not persuade him to accept this precautionary measure. They begged and pleaded and wheedled, but the Prince wouldn't budge an inch.

Finally Jack McCurdy strode over and smacked one of his huge hands on Edward's shoulder in fatherly fashion.

"Damn it to hell, Prince," he said affectionately, "we don't want to *lose* you!"

His Royal Highness looked startled for a moment, and then obediently walked over to have the guide snub him securely before venturing into the Nipigon.

It seems to take long seasoning in the lonely places to develop the authentic wilderness character. Perhaps, with the spectacular advances which have been made in communications of all kinds in the wilderness in recent years, that certain mysterious conditioner which helped create the backwoods character no longer quite functions. Yesterday's far greater isolation must surely have been an important factor in creating him. There was so much more elbowroom in which individualism could grow and flourish.

It may be that, like the rest of us whose names are now filed by numbers in the places where we work and in the capitals from which we are governed, even those highly individualistic personalities once found in the north are at last surrendering to uniformity. Some of them may still be found there, but they grow old, and soon may be no more.

Up in Dawson City Alex Evans used to proudly show visitors around the Palace Grand Opera House (the original one the government tore down to make way for the expensive and carefully constructed replica that was built in 1962 for the Gold Rush Festival). The old one was sagging and dusty and weatherbeaten with the grey of neglect, but something had seeped deeply into its walls, something from the roistering days when Dawson boasted the largest population west of Winnipeg. Alex had been there when it all happened back in 1898 and he loved the Palace Grand and loved to tell visitors about it and the city of dreams where it stood.

"The streets would be full of men, thousands of them," he would recall. "But you would seldom see an angry blow struck and there was never a man murdered in Dawson. There was something we all shared and that was hardship, and there was something about the sharing of it that made us respect each other and what property we had.

"I've lived here ever since the Klondike rush and it was always the same until not long ago. I could have left my watch on the table, if I wanted to, and gone into the hills for weeks, with my door wide open. When I came back my watch would have still been lying there, ready to wind up and put back in my pocket—but then they built the new road and things got different. Around 1944, I went out and bought me a lock."

Alex's little cabin was snug enough and when you sat there beside the stove with him he would declare there was still lots of gold to be found in the creeks if only there were men left with the guts and passion to go out there and look for it. You gathered that Alex himself still had the guts and the passion but no longer had the legs for it. He was growing very old, with a voice that quavered when he talked. He spoke of the Klondike rush as though it had happened only months before. I asked him if he'd ever known Robert W. Service, the Bard of the Yukon, and he allowed that he had.

"He was knowed," said Alex, "as the biggest bum in the Yukon! He used to work in the bank and they didn't pay him much and he used to borrow from us fellers all the time."

It was plain that Alex wasn't impressed by any smart-pants bank clerk who went around writing poetry, even though the world-famed bard was then living comfortably on his royalties in a villa on the Mediterranean.

Just a few days before they opened the completely rebuilt Palace Grand, Alex Evans died in the Old Men's Home in Dawson City and he never did get to see the great official ceremonies, with the dignitaries arriving in dinner jackets to attend the first night of a genuine Broadway play called "Foxy." Perhaps it was just as well, because Alex, in his way, was the ghost of the old Palace Grand and ghosts don't seem to thrive in replicas of such places, no matter how authentically the work of reconstruction may have been done.

In Aklavik (Eskimo for Place of the Bear) they look down with heavy scorn upon Inuvik (Eskimo for Place of the Man), the new town thirty-two miles to the east. They call it Toytown, because from the air its brightly painted, uniform dwellings do look a little bit like doll-houses set out on display on a department store counter. In Inuvik's only hotel, bearing the impressive name of the Mackenzie Arms, you can see an Eskimo in full native regalia quaffing a martini in a cocktail bar as dimly lit and streamlined as most any slinky bistro you'd find in the south.

Years ago Aklavik was pronounced by highly qualified government engineers to be sinking into the silt of the Mackenzie River delta. But it's still there, even though some of its larger buildings do seem to be staggering a bit and some of its smaller shacks on the banks of the muddy Mackenzie could almost be mistaken for dog-houses, if dogs had houses in that stark country. One spring a great flood hit Aklavik. The water was so high and fast that it carried one of the community's churches right down the river, floating upright, with its bell ringing mournfully as the building swayed in the current on its way to the Arctic Ocean.

But even this setback failed to change the minds of those stubborn holdouts in Aklavik who had refused to move to Toytown.

"It didn't hurt us none," a loyal oldtimer told me. "A little flushin' out does a town like this a lot of good now and then."

It is my impression, after several visits to Aklavik, that just about all of the residents who remain there are what might be called characters. There was probably something about the exodus to Inuvik of the more genteel citizens that left a sort of hard core of characters among that staunch and hardy band who refused to move.

One such was Anker Hoydahl.

I met him back in 1962 in Aklavik as he was awaiting the arrival of a bush plane that was to pick him up, with his gear, and fly him to a base camp for his annual prospecting expedition. He was a soft-spoken, friendly man, nearing seventy, and he'd spent most of his life searching for gold. At first he'd done it all on foot, carrying just about everything he owned with him. He would disappear in the early summer and no one in Aklavik would hear from him or worry about him, for that matter, until the fall.

He claimed he had once carried a whole stove on his back, along with his food and other prospecting equipment, for 125 miles.

"Mind you," said he with a grin, "it was only one of those little bitsy sheet metal stoves, but it began to feel heavier than a whole damned kitchen range by the time I'd been carrying it a few days!"

The stove was worth carrying, he explained, when you were out for a long spell, because it could be set up right in the tent at his base camp to keep a man snug and warm and dry during those chill wet days that can come to the Arctic in midsummer, even though it might be hot enough to fairly cook you at other times in July and August. Campfires might be all right for side trips, but for long spells a stove was the thing. So he carried one on his back across all that rock and muskeg.

But now, said Anker happily, the airplane had changed all that. It could whisk him into his base camp in an hour. In all his years of looking he hadn't yet turned up anything really important. He picked up a bit of gold dust and a few small nuggets during the year, but just enough to barely pay his way.

"Supposing," I asked him, "you really struck it rich this year. Would you go outside and buy yourself a mansion on a hill in a big city?"

Anker thought it over for a while.

"I've often wondered about that," said he. "Sometimes I think the search for the stuff is the thing I really enjoy. You never know when you might strike it—around the next bend in the river—through the next pass in the mountains—it's mighty nice to always have something you're looking for. Maybe if I found it, I wouldn't be happy any more."

Anker Hoydahl's search came to an end very soon after I had been talking to him. The bush plane that picked him up next day for the trip into his base camp crashed in the Mackenzie Mountains, killing Anker while he still had something to look for.

A few of these wilderness nomads did, of course, find what they were looking for, to Canada's great benefit. One of them was my friend Marius Kristian Madsen, with whom I often fished and hunted before his death in 1967. He was a burly, stubborn man, who before he was twenty had faced enough hardship and adventure to last most men a lifetime. When he died in Toronto at the age of sixty-six, he was a multimillionaire, with such monuments to his name as the great Madsen Red Lake gold mine in Northwestern Ontario and a nearby community called Madsen. His other interests ranged from gravel pits and real estate developments in the Toronto area to a luxurious resort hotel in Jamaica. In other words, he made it big.

Marius Madsen's life of wilderness adventure really began on June 8, 1920, when he set sail from Copenhagen in his native Denmark with fifteen other men in the 120-foot schooner *Dagny* on an expedition to the Arctic for the Danish East Greenland Company. He was only nineteen and the youngest member of the party.

The *Dagny* was bound for the east coast of Greenland, where the expedition hoped to gather additional information on the geology and the flora and fauna of the bleak country, as well as bring back some specimens of wildlife for use by museums and universities.

Thirty-five miles off Shannon Island, at the mouth of Ardencaple Fjord, near the seventy-fifth degree of north latitude, the *Dagny* became trapped in the pack ice and was slowly ground to destruction. Hauling on sleds what supplies they could salvage from the wrecked vessel before she slid down into the sea through a gap in the ice, the